COLOR STYLE

COLOR STYLE

HOW TO IDENTIFY THE COLORS THAT ARE RIGHT FOR YOUR HOME

CAROLYN WARRENDER

ABBEVILLE PRESS   PUBLISHERS

NEW YORK LONDON PARIS

FOR OUR CHILDREN
Jamie and Geordie
Francis, Rollo and Zoe

First published in the United States of America in 1996 by
Abbeville Press, 488 Madison Avenue, New York, N.Y. 10022.

Special photography by Shona Wood
Color wheel illustrations by Cherrill Parris
Practical illustrations by John Hutchinson
Picture research by Julia Pashley

First edition
10 9 8 7 6 5 4 3 2

ISBN 0-7892-0255-7

Although we warrant the accuracy and reliability of the instructions
given for the projects described in this book, we cannot assume any
responsibility or liability for the results of the projects or any
consequential loss or damage suffered from their use. While every
care has been taken with the printing of the color wheels, the
publisher cannot guarantee total accuracy in every case.

CONTENTS

INTRODUCTION

Imagine that you are returning home after a long summer holiday. What happens when you turn the key in the lock and walk around the house or apartment, making sure that everything is in place? Do you feel a sense of satisfaction and well-being as you move from room to room, or does a checklist start to form in your mind—I need to replace that carpet; I must do something about the lighting in the living room; how can I make the kitchen more cheerful? As likely as not, you will experience a mixture of positive and negative emotions as you make your tour. Most of us decorate our homes over a period of several years and, during that time, new styles and fashions influence us. We also make fresh discoveries about ourselves. Even the most seasoned interior designers will look for ways to alter and improve their homes as they move through them.

Home decoration is an ongoing process. In this book, I hope to share with you the ways in which I have made that process one that is rich in adventure, enjoyment and discovery. My starting point, and the point to which I return again and again, is color. How can the home owner of today make the most of color? There is certainly no shortage of material with which to experiment—if anything, there is too much. Decorating shops offer the consumer a dazzling range of paints, wallpapers, soft furnishing fabrics, stencil patterns, carpets, rugs and storage systems. What's more, there is a huge range of international styles on the market. Today's buyer can select tables from Singapore, beds and wardrobes from Scandinavia, Shaker-style kitchens, Mediterranean-style bathrooms. With such a vast array of colors and traditions to choose from, it can be extremely hard to establish your own personal style. How can you experiment with the materials that are on the market without making costly mistakes and ending up with a jumble of styles? And how can you acquire the skills that will give you the confidence to create a house that reflects your particular personality and taste?

I believe that you, and anyone else, can acquire these skills by learning, first, what colors will work best for you and secondly, how to combine these colors so that they bring out the best features in your home. Just as you are likely to feel more cheerful and confident in clothes whose color and style flatter you, so you are likely to feel more at ease in surroundings that enhance you.

The first step is to establish your color palette. When I use color in interior design, I take my inspiration from the natural world. The elements of nature seem to provide everything you need to create color schemes that are harmonious, versatile and enjoyable to live with. So the seven palettes I use are all based on the elements. They are:

The Natural Palette, the Air Palette, the Wind Palette, the Water Palette, the Fire Palette, the Earth Palette and the Mineral Palette.

Within each of these palettes, the colors are subdivided into warm-based and cool-based. Warm-based colors have a yellow base, while cool-based colors have a blue base. And by studying the first chapter of this book and then completing the questionnaire on pages 124–25, you will be able to ascertain which color palette is the best for you. With this as your foundation, you will know how to make the most of the information in Living with Color, the central section of the book (see page 62). Here, you will learn about the ways in which color, light and texture interact with each other, and you will be shown how to experiment with different colors and textures by making your own sample boards. You will also learn how to view your house as a whole, and so create a color scheme that is coordinated in an overall sense. Then a room-by-room analysis will show you how the different components of a room can be combined in colorways that work alongside each other to achieve a particular atmosphere. For each room in the house, a step-by-step project will enable you to create some of these effects for yourself, without needing to employ an interior designer.

I hope that this book will give you the skills you need to use color with confidence, flair and pleasure and that it will be both a source of inspiration and a practical reference work for many years to come.

Carolyn Warrender, London, 1996

Understanding Color

The language of color is not difficult to master. You can quickly learn the principles established by major artists and color theorists in previous eras and apply them to interior design. Whatever your budget, you can use color to transform the dreariest of rooms into a place fit for a queen. Today more than ever before, you have the advantage of a wonderful range of fabrics, paints, wallpapers and accessories. Once you have learned the basic rules of color and identified your own palette, you will be able to use this rich array of materials with flair, confidence and natural good taste.

THE COLOR SPECTRUM

When we perceive different colors, what we are really seeing is light reflected back to our eyes in different wavelengths from the variety of surfaces around us.

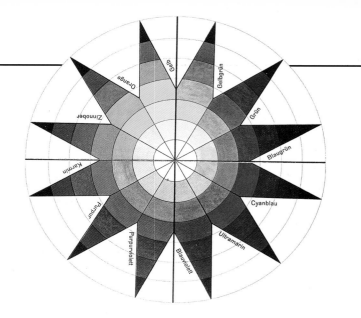

ABOVE Johannes Itten's color star defines the twelve colors (hues) by tone (light or dark) and saturation (depth of color).

The wavelengths that together make up the colors of the rainbow—red, orange, yellow, green, indigo and violet— are traditionally regarded as comprising the color spectrum. Red has the longest wavelength and violet the shortest, with the wavelengths of the colors in between steadily decreasing.

At either end of the spectrum are white and black. White reflects and contains all the other colors within it, as Sir Isaac Newton discovered in 1666. He used a triangular prism to catch a shaft of sunlight and found that he created a second shaft that showed each color of the rainbow contained within the white sunlight. In contrast to white, black absorbs light. The three pigments used by printers— cyan (blue), yellow and magenta (red)—combine to create black as a fourth color in the printing process.

PRIMARY, SECONDARY AND TERTIARY COLORS

Just over a hundred years after Newton's discovery, the scientist and naturalist Moses Harris created in 1770 the first color wheel to classify red, blue and yellow as the three primary colors. (The primary colors are so called because they cannot be created by mixing any other colors together.) By the mid-nineteenth century this classification was widely accepted by artists. Then, in the early twentieth century, the German painter, teacher and art theoretician Johannes Itten extended the classification to include secondary and tertiary colors. In the 1920s Itten was an important personality in the early German Bauhaus movement, which aimed to incorporate art into everyday life, including industrial life. Itten played a key role in pioneering a new approach to color. During the 1920s, he developed a color star that featured twelve colors: three primary, three secondary and six tertiary. The secondary colors are made by mixing two of the primary colors together—red and yellow make orange; yellow and blue make green; and red and blue make purple. The six tertiary colors are created when two secondary colors are mixed together.

TINTS AND SHADES

Any color can be lightened by the addition of white; it is then known as a tint. The same color can also be darkened by the addition of black, known as shading. Red, when tinted with white, becomes a feminine pink; when shaded with black it turns to a more masculine burgundy. The addition of white and black to different colors is said to change that color's tone.

COMPLEMENTARY AND HARMONIOUS COLORS

Complementary colors have a strong visual resonance when they are placed alongside each other. Red and green are complementaries, as are blue and yellow, and orange and purple. When you use complementary colors in interior design, you should include both colors in equal measure and of an equal intensity to achieve a balanced result.

Harmonious colors rest alongside each other in the color spectrum. Yellow and orange harmonize with each other, as do blue and purple. Experimenting with crayons is an easy way to explore the relationship of different colors to each other and discover which combinations you like.

LEFT This stone-flagged hallway shows four harmonious colors comfortably juxtaposed. The wood of the staircase is close in the color spectrum to that of the flagstones, while the pink of the wall contains sufficient beige to link the two. The white painted baseboard extends the floor area, adding light and space.

THE COLOR PALETTES

Johannes Itten also pioneered the notion of warm and cool colors. According to Itten, any shade of color can have either a warm base or a cool base, an insight with considerable implications for interior designers. If you know whether you prefer a cool yellow or a warm yellow as the background color for your room, and if you know how to extend that color scheme according to Itten's classification, you are well on the way to creating the kind of room you want. Itten divided the color spectrum into two complementary halves, one half comprising warm shades and the other comprising cool shades. Similarly, the color wheel shown opposite divides the shades into warm and cool colors. At the same time, it shows each of the colors at varying degrees of intensity and depth. The warm and cool halves of the wheel are subdivided into seven distinct palettes. Because much of my inspiration comes from the natural world, I call these palettes Natural, Air, Wind, Water, Fire, Earth and Mineral. Thus, within the divisions of warm and cool are:

THE NATURAL PALETTE
THE AIR PALETTE
THE WIND PALETTE
THE WATER PALETTE
THE FIRE PALETTE
THE EARTH PALETTE
THE MINERAL PALETTE

These seven color palettes will give you the tools you need to extend your color scheme in a way that is visually harmonious. Later in this chapter, each of the color palettes is discussed in more detail. The following chapter presents many examples of color palettes combined in specific ways to create a wide range of effects and styles in all rooms of the home. Answering the questionnaire in the final chapter of the book will help you to find which color palette will work best for you. For example, if the Wind Palette is most appropriate for you, it is a good idea to combine your decorating colors from the shades that are specific to that palette. In this way, you will be able to design and to decorate your home to suit your personal taste. In particu-

ABOVE Cool colors, based on blue undertones

lar, you will be able confidently to combine a variety of colors in such a way that each room in your home is well balanced, harmonious and a pleasure to live in. As you gain more confidence, you will find that you can combine warm and cool colors from the same palettes as well as working exclusively within one half of the spectrum. For example, you can use warm accents as highlights in a primarily cool color scheme. Remember too that the natural palette can be combined with any of the other six.

ABOVE Warm colors, based on yellow undertones

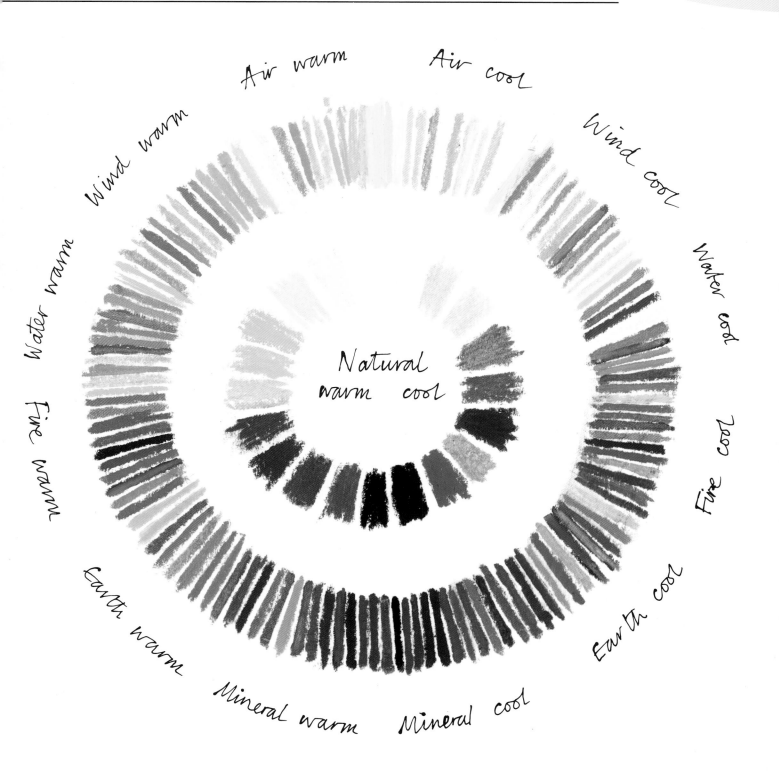

THE PROPERTIES OF COLOR

RED

Red is a color that advances, stimulating a response and creating an atmosphere of assertion and strength. It is associated with excitement, vitality and physical power. Because it is a color that flatters the skin, it can make an excellent background in rooms that are used for social functions. Pale pinks are warm and peaceful and combine successfully with greens. The deeper reds can create an atmosphere of restrained opulence and power.

ORANGE

Midway between red and yellow, orange is essentially a cheerful color, with a glow that can be used to good effect in north- and east-facing rooms. Since it is also an assertive and dynamic color, it can be overpowering when used on large surfaces in interior design, though used with discretion it can create an atmosphere of vivacious spontaneity and liveliness.

YELLOW

Because we tend to associate it with sunshine, yellow can appear as a light source in its own right. This makes it an effective color for bringing a sense of natural light into urban settings; even dark yellow rooms can have an airy, radiant atmosphere. The use of yellow in any living space can create a feeling of hope and inspiration, and an optimistic sense that all is well with the world.

GREEN

A discreet color, green suggests security, protection and harmony. Green also has a calming effect, making it a popular choice for bedrooms, while dark greens make excellent colors for studies and home offices. The greenrooms of theaters are so called because their green walls are intended to steady the nerves of actors and actresses as they prepare to perform on stage. Pale greens are particularly restful, though they can be severe on the skin; a reliable way to counteract this is by introducing rich blues and turquoises somewhere in the room as color accents.

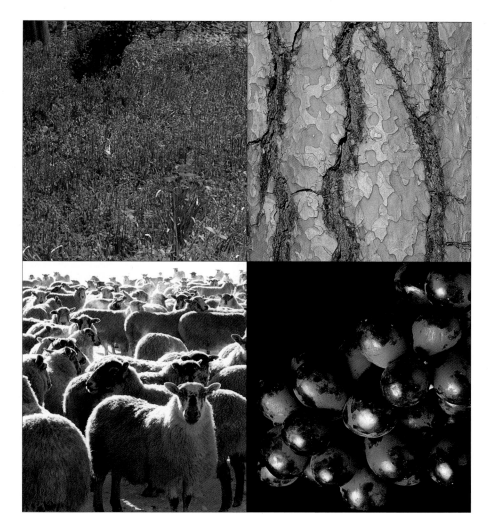

many shades and textures of brown that combine in the bark of a tree or the shell of a nut are infinitely rich and subtle and extraordinarily restful to look upon. Some of these qualities are captured in well-made furniture, turning the best wooden pieces into collectors' items. One characteristic of brown is that it creates a feeling of coolness and warmth at the same time. As a furnishing fabric, it combines well with rich colors such as purple and gold, a popular combination in the Victorian era.

WHITE

White promotes an air of cleanliness, simplicity and hygiene. In buildings with strong architectural features, such as exposed beams, white can be used to give these features additional emphasis. However, it is often seen as a "safe" fallback where a stronger color would be more effective. If you are decorating a room with a white background, you run the risk of creating a clinical atmosphere, so consider choosing an off-white such as gardenia, ivory or dove gray to create a softer and more finished look.

BLACK

Because it absorbs light, black is an exacting color to work with in interior design. And its association with bereavement and death can make it seem morbid for the home. However, black accents can transform an otherwise bland interior; black picture frames and curtain rails, burgundy-black lacquer and black lampshades will introduce a note of drama and sophistication into otherwise plain surroundings. Black will also punctuate color schemes that rely on strong contrasting colors.

BLUE

The color of the sea and sky, blue has a quality of cool expansiveness and openness. Used in interior design, it has a relaxing and sedative effect. Blue is associated with a sense of formality, though the midblues also have a playful quality about them. Because of its association with water, blue is a popular color for kitchens and bathrooms; it can also create an atmosphere of spaciousness and tranquility in reception rooms and a fresh look, combined with white, in bedrooms.

VIOLET

A combination of blue and red, violet is a regal and dignified color that needs to be used with discretion. Pale shades of violet are restful and serene, but the darker shades can make it difficult to focus and, if used over large expanses, are tiring on the eyes. At the same time, this quality can make purple an excellent foil for works of art.

BROWN

The color of living wood, brown is essentially an earth color. In nature, the

A COLOR BY ANY OTHER NAME

The human eye can recognize thousands of shades in the colors we term generically as red, yellow, blue and so on. Remember, though, that wallpaper, paint and textile manufacturers may well give products containing similar shades quite different names. When you are trying to find a color that you like, it can be confusing to find what seems to be the same shade classified by one manufacturer as forest green, by another as jungle green, and by a third as oak green. It can also be dangerous to assume that a paint called pale apricot will complement a fabric of the same name. The best way to negotiate the maze of color names on the market is to collect samples and make your own assessment of what colors work well with each other. The names I have chosen for the palettes described here are all inspired by the colors of nature.

LEFT Yellow is famous for its uplifting properties and is most effective in spaces that enjoy plenty of natural light. On this stairwell its effectiveness is enhanced by the yellow panes in the stained glass window.

RIGHT Red is a warm and inviting color. It is softened when combined with cream and given definition when combined with black. This sitting room employs both of these combinations, with an attractive mixture of patterns adding to the overall effect.

HOW COLOR AFFECTS US

Using color is a two-way process. We use it to express our personalities, to make statements about how we see ourselves and to reveal our preferences and tastes. At the same time, the colors we live with directly influence the way we feel, the efficiency with which we work and the extent to which we are able to relax. Color can play a major part in our overall state of well-being. So whether you want to create a dramatic living room or a subdued bedroom, knowing how to combine different shades of color within a color spectrum that is almost infinitely expandable will enable you to create genuinely personal color schemes with confidence, individuality and flair. The qualities associated with different colors are discussed on pages 14–15, but remember that the many tones of any given color can achieve quite varied effects. For each color, there are thousands of varieties on the market in the form of paint, wallpaper and soft furnishing fabrics. In order to achieve the look you want, you need to pay close attention to the shades of color you select.

COLOR AND SPACE

Color can significantly alter the sense of space in a room. Dark shades will make a large room seem smaller, while light and neutral colors will increase the sense of space in a small room. So by choosing to decorate a room with a dark or light color tone, you will immediately create a particular effect. Before making your choice, consider the purpose of the room you are decorating. Is this a space where you wish to create a quiet, introspective atmosphere or one that is more stimulating and lively, appropriate for entertaining? In contemporary homes, many rooms are used for more than one purpose. When decorating a bedroom, for example, consider whether the room is also going to function as a play area for a child, or a study area for a teenager.

COLOR AND LIGHT

Because color *is* light, changes in light bring about immediate changes in the color of any object or surface. Conversely, the atmosphere of a room can be altered dramatically by the introduction of a new color because that color will alter the quality of light in the room. In creating a successful scheme in any room, it is essential to bear in mind the intimate relationship between color and light. Which way does the room face? How much sunlight does it receive, and at what time of day? When is the room most

ABOVE In this sitting room the discipline of white and lavender dominates the color scheme. But the use of several textures—on the rug, chairs, blinds, curtains and paintwork—enhances the interplay of color and light.

likely to be used? To what extent does the quality of natural light in the room change from season to season? When illuminated by artificial light, how does the interplay between light and color change? And how do you, as the architect of the room, wish it to change?

ABOVE The almost exclusive use of natural colors, with two glazed Japanese pots as accents, creates an atmosphere of simple elegance in this music room.

Light alone can transform a room without any other alterations. It can make spaces seem larger or smaller, more functional or more intimate. By making the most of natural light, and by using artificial light not only for illumination but also for a particular effect, you can make the same living space extraordinarily versatile. If you use your kitchen as a dining room, for example, you will need to consider how you can explore the many different ways of using light to change the mood of the room at different times of day.

COLOR AND CONTRAST

Because of the interplay of color and light, contrasting textures can create many pleasingly subtle effects when you are working either with the same color or with different ones. Contrasts such as rough-smooth, pointed-blunt, light-dark, hard-soft, heavy-light can all enrich the color treatment of an interior space.

NATURAL COLORS

Natural is the term used to describe any color in which white has been used as a tint to dilute the impact of that color. The natural colors most often used in interior design are gray-based or brown-based. The notion of a natural red or a natural blue sounds contradictory, but if these or any other colors are predominantly white, then they can be regarded as natural too.

THE FUNCTION OF NATURALS

In many ways, naturals are the designer's best friend. Used exclusively, they create a restful, calm and undemanding ambience. As a base color on floors, walls and ceilings, they provide a foil for the impact of more dramatic soft furnishing fabrics. Naturals can also be combined with stronger colors such as reds and oranges in patterned rugs and carpets, to bridge the contrast between a solid foreground color, such as a red sofa, and a neutral base color, such as dove-gray walls.

Natural colors lend a sense of space to small rooms. They can be dreary in basements or north-facing rooms, but wherever there is plenty of natural light, the dominance of white in naturals will be very effective.

THE
NATURAL
PALETTE

THE NATURAL PALETTE

The natural palette divides into warm and cool base colors.
Once you have completed the questionnaire on pages
124–25, and have discovered if you are essentially warm-
or cool-based, use the appropriate wheel to select your
colors. These can then be used in decorating or furnishing
your room, either on their own or in combination with
colors from the warm or cool side of the other palettes.

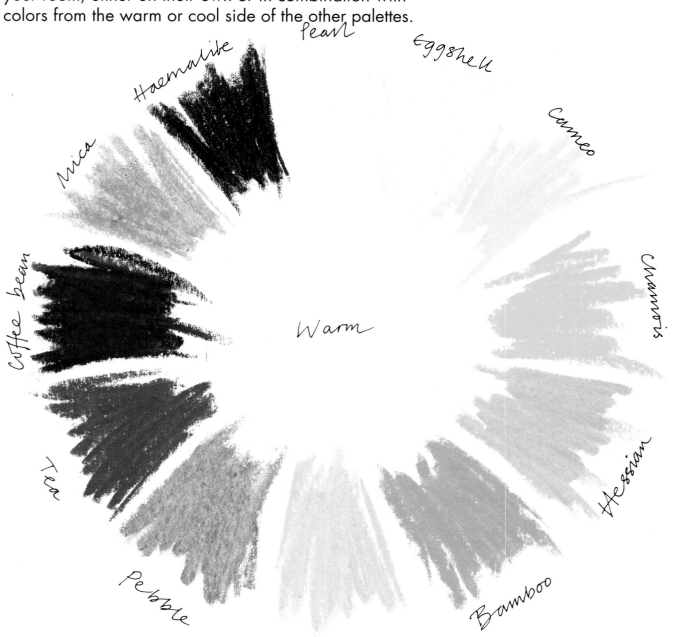

Pearl

Eggshell

Haematite

Cameo

Mica

Chamois

Coffee bean

Warm

Hessian

Tea

Bamboo

Pebble

Acorn

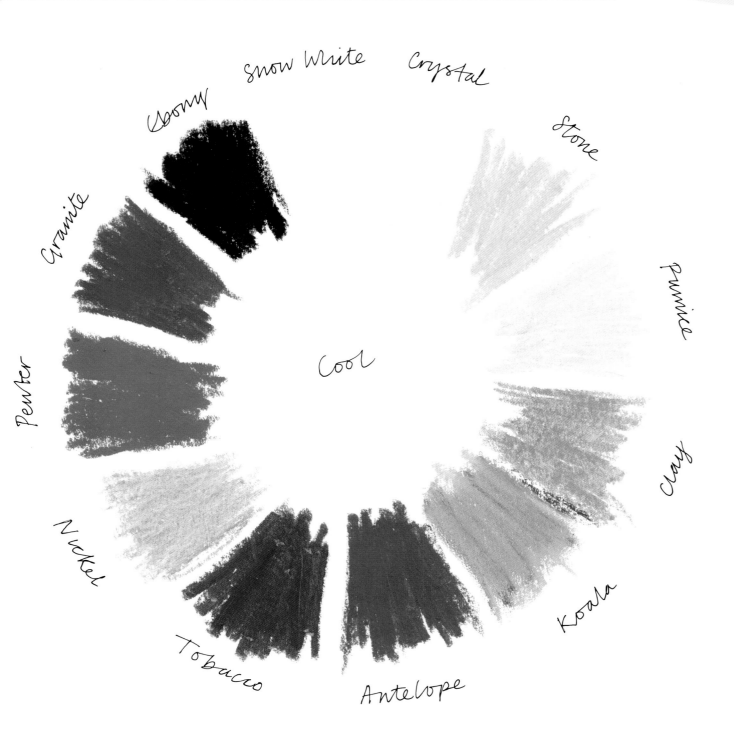

Ebony

Snow White

Crystal

Stone

Granite

Pumice

Pewter

Cool

Clay

Nickel

Koala

Tobacco

Antelope

Natural describes any color in which black, brown or white is the main ingredient. The natural colors that are most often used in home furnishings are gray-based or brown-based. Like the kitchen cupboard in which you keep all the basics you need for cooking, the natural palette is full of basics. Look upon natural colors in the same way as that cupboard when planning your color schemes. Among naturals you will find the shades that act as a foil for more intense colors. Think about how natural colors appear on a beach, with sand and pebbles acting as a base for the deep sea and rock colors. All naturals have a pleasing simplicity about them, which is perhaps the reason why they find favor in so many people's homes. If you are uncertain about how to experiment with color, the natural palette can be a good place to start. Used exclusively, these colors will create a restful, calm and undemanding ambience. As a base color on floors, walls and ceilings, they provide a foil for the impact of more dramatic furnishings. Think too of using naturals as accents for scatter cushions, trimmings and rugs in more colorful rooms. The joy of natural colors is that they can be used with any color you want. They lend a sense of space to small and dark rooms. Where there is plenty of natural light, they will enhance that light. Naturals are also a good choice for any well-lit room where you want an atmosphere of spaciousness, simplicity and calm. They are excellent colors for hallways and corridors, as they will both link and punctuate the overall scheme in a home.

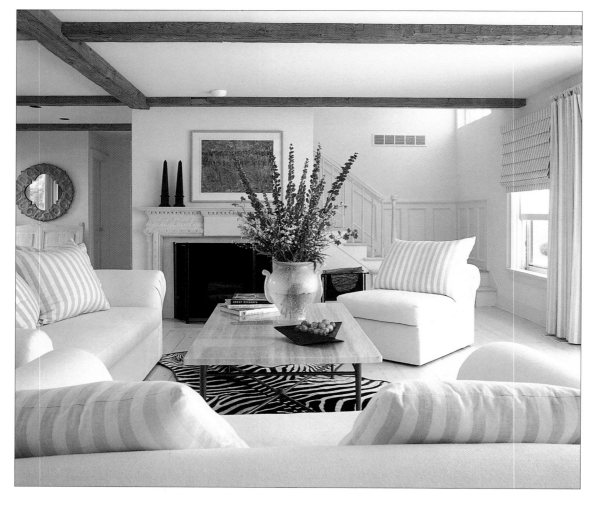

LEFT Cool whites used across the floor, walls and ceilings dissolve angles and borders. In this room, their use also accentuates the importance of the exposed beams. The striped cushion covers add a touch of definition, but the theme here is definitely one of "less is more."

RIGHT Large urns with bold displays of twigs stand in this room like two silent guests. These warm natural colors and the contrasting textures of the coir matting, woodwork, sofa, stoneware and cushions give this room a marked tactile quality.

THE
AIR
PALETTE

THE AIR PALETTE

The air palette divides into warm and cool base colors.
Once you have completed the questionnaire on pages
124–25, and have discovered if you are essentially warm-
or cool-based, use the appropriate wheel to select your
colors. These can then be used in decorating or furnishing
your room, either on their own or in combination with
colors from the warm or cool side of the other palettes.

Vanilla

Cloud

Sunray

Oyster

Pollen

Feather

Warm

Solstice

Evensong

Dawn

Mist

Vapour

High Noon

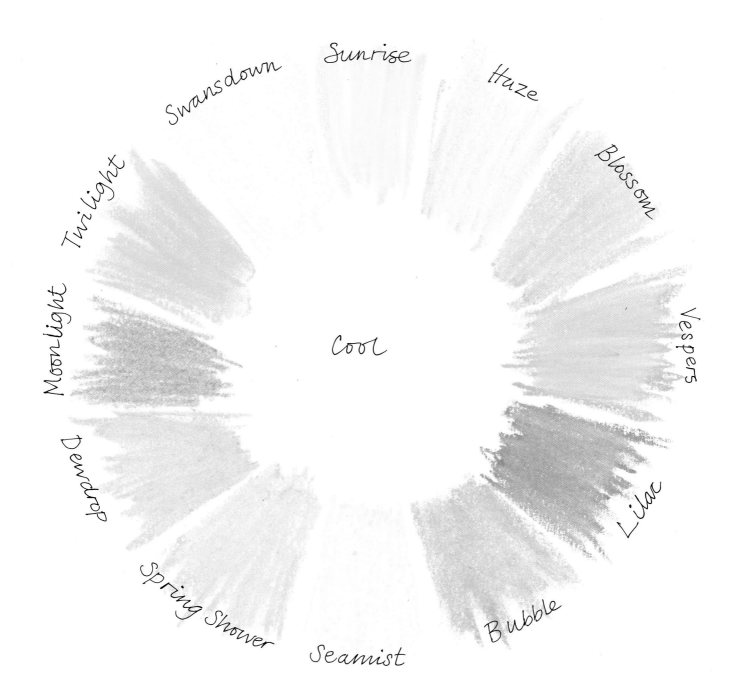

Sunrise

Swansdown

Haze

Twilight

Blossom

Moonlight

Vespers

Cool

Dewdrop

Lilac

Spring Shower

Bubble

Seamist

Air is around us all the time. We say the sky is blue, but what color is the air itself? Like the element from which it takes its name, the air color palette is subtle and elusive. More than any other palette, these colors are suffused with light, giving them an attractive outdoor allure with very feminine, calm and summery tones.

Among the warm air colors are Sunray, Pollen, Mist and Cloud. Among the cool air colors are Haze, Bubble, Dewdrop and Swansdown. There is a romantic association to these colors that makes them ideal for bedrooms, guest rooms and bathrooms. At the same time, the outdoor quality of the palette is suitable for rooms in which plants play a major role in the color scheme. The air colors also make good companions for patterned fabrics, especially when the patterns are understated.

The delicacy of the air palette can easily be overpowered by dark colors and by heavy pieces of furniture. With these colors, consider using painted and stenciled furniture, perhaps coordinating a motif from a floral curtain or bedspread as part of your scheme. Pale woods such as ash, bamboo and pine rest well alongside the warm air colors, while limed oak complements the cool air colors on the other side of the palette. Choose lightweight curtain fabrics such as muslins, soft cottons, delicate silks and chintz to make the best of air colors.

The air palette belongs, above all, in rooms that receive plenty of natural light. If you are converting an attic space into a young girl's den, or creating a light-filled bedroom in a country cottage, this palette will help you to achieve an atmosphere that gives a sense of airy, sunny spaciousness.

RIGHT Warm yellows act as the foreground colors in this wood-paneled sitting room. The discipline of yellow and white is lightly accented by blue and green, creating the spirit of a sunny garden.

RIGHT Cool air colors create a distinctive, feminine atmosphere in this bedroom. The choice of a finely detailed pattern on the quilt and the abundance of lace pillowcases add to this effect.

THE
WIND
PALETTE

THE WIND PALETTE

The wind palette divides into warm and cool base colors.
Once you have completed the questionnaire on pages
124–25, and have discovered if you are essentially warm-
or cool-based, use the appropriate wheel to select your
colors. These can then be used in decorating or furnishing
your room, either on their own or in combination with
colors from the warm or cool side of the other palettes.

Broom

Shadow

Peach

Silver Birch

Sandstorm

Lichen

Persimmon

Warm

Sirocco

Coral Reef

Azure

Rosewood

Rosa Mundi

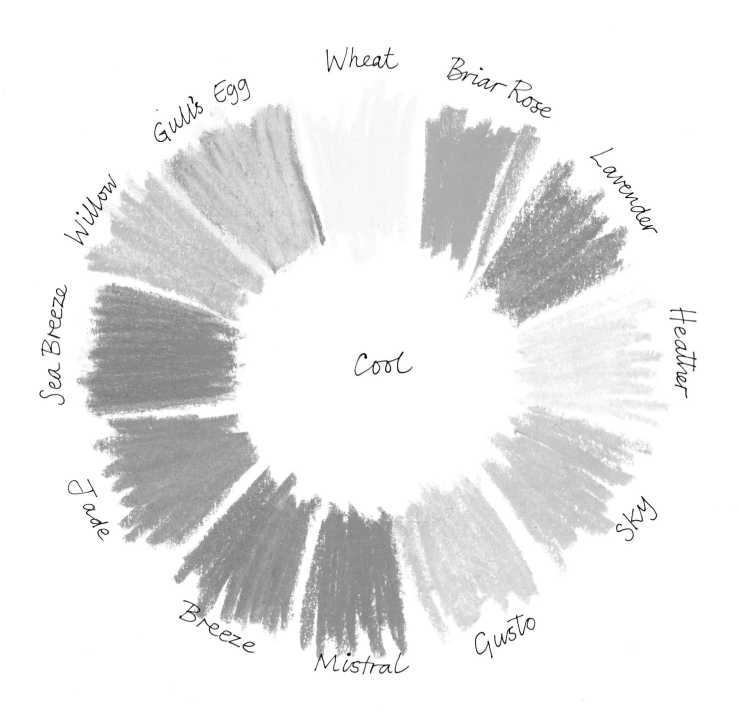

Wind immediately evokes a sense of movement and change, and successful color schemes based on the wind palette do the same. This palette can be used anywhere in the home. Wind rooms are relaxed, with an emphasis on flexibility; never boring, they lend themselves to a combination of patterns and plains. They are a dependable choice in any room where you want the atmosphere to be inviting and interesting, without being too dramatic.

The wind palette is soft, welcoming and invigorating. These colors lie midway between the pastels that characterize the air palette and the clarity and depth of the water palette. This gives them a subtlety and at the same time a particularly versatile quality. To make the most of the wind colors, choose a combination of several shades to work together in the same room.

From the warm side of the palette, create a color scheme using Sirocco, Shadow and Clover or, if working with the cool colors, try using Sky and Heather together.

Planning color schemes with wind colors is a joy because, subtle as they may appear, they also possess a quiet gaiety that is easy on the eye and restful to live with but at the same time encourages experimentation. With this palette you can be quite adventurous in your choice of patterns and colors since it can withstand quite bold and highly patterned designs, combined with richly colored rugs and pictures. Remember too that you can use the softer natural colors as a base or as accents to complete your color scheme. Wind colors work well in rooms of any aspect and add definition to small spaces. A combination of them reinforces the sense of movement.

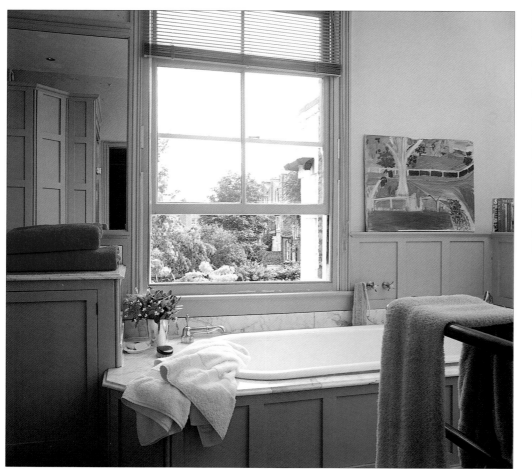

LEFT The division between indoors and out is reduced by choosing cool greens that pick up the colors of the foliage outside the bathroom of this suburban home.

RIGHT The warm yellows of the wind palette provide a strong background color for a collection of prints. The brass bedstead enriches the effect of the yellow paintwork, while the floral pattern of the counterpane gives the room a fresh, summery atmosphere.

THE
WATER
PALETTE

THE WATER PALETTE

The water palette divides into warm and cool base colors.
Once you have completed the questionnaire on pages
124–25, and have discovered if you are essentially warm-
or cool-based, use the appropriate wheel to select your
colors. These can then be used in decorating or furnishing
your room, either on their own or in combination with
colors from the warm or cool side of the other palettes.

Sand

Dune

Peridot

Ochre

Seaspray

Atoll

Warm

Aquamarine

Cayenne

Spa

Periwinkle

Sea Anemone

Jasper

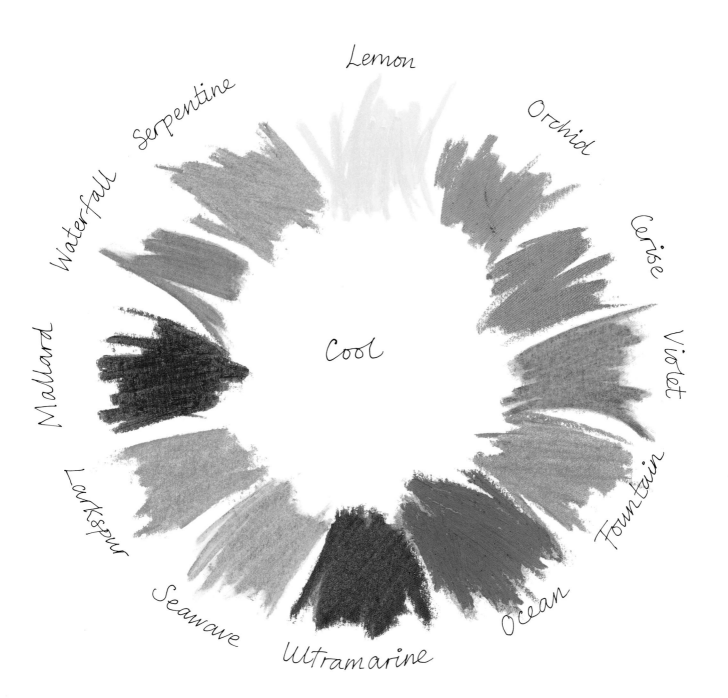

Lemon

Serpentine

Orchid

Waterfall

Cerise

Mallard

Violet

Cool

Fountain

Larkspur

Seawave

Ocean

Ultramarine

Waterfalls, rivers, oceans, rain showers and snowfall—water is the element that flows through and around, constantly changing its form. But whatever form it comes in, water is like an empty container for light, making it an element whose hallmark is clarity.

Whether warm or cool, the colors of the water palette all share this quality of clarity and depth. They have a crispness that makes you want to use them in a way that reflects an uncluttered, happy home. The water colors combine beautifully with the stark simplicity of Pearl and Snowflake in the natural palette, especially in bathrooms and kitchens. Water colors have a vividness and energy that can make for effective color schemes based on using only one or two colors alongside each other.

From the cool side of the palette, Waterfall, Fountain and Ultramarine make great bathroom colors. If using the warm category, try coordinating Jasper, Periwinkle and Spa, for example, to establish a successful color scheme in a living room.

If you are tempted to focus on one particular color from the water palette in order to maximize its impact, remember that you can increase the effect by using coordinating tones of the same color as accents. For example, use Mallard as a main room color, with Waterfall and Serpentine as the accent colors. Small details like painting a recess or the woodwork in a coordinating or a contrasting color will give your color scheme a touch of flair and individuality.

LEFT Cool, minty greens enliven the walls of this dining room and provide an assertive background for the display of plates and prints, and contrast with the dark wood of the antique cabinet.

RIGHT The division of this wall space into large expanses of warm blue and yellow gives this bathroom a note of understated elegance, an effect increased by the use of sponging as a paint effect.

THE
FIRE
PALETTE

THE FIRE PALETTE

The fire palette divides into warm and cool base colors.
Once you have completed the questionnaire on pages
124–25, and have discovered if you are essentially warm-
or cool-based, use the appropriate wheel to select your
colors. These can then be used in decorating or furnishing
your room, either on their own or in combination with
colors from the warm or cool side of the other palettes.

Sunshine

Cactus

Marigold

Grass

Cyclamen

Tourmaline

Flame

Warm

Turquoise

Geranium

Cornflower

Hyacinth

Delphinium

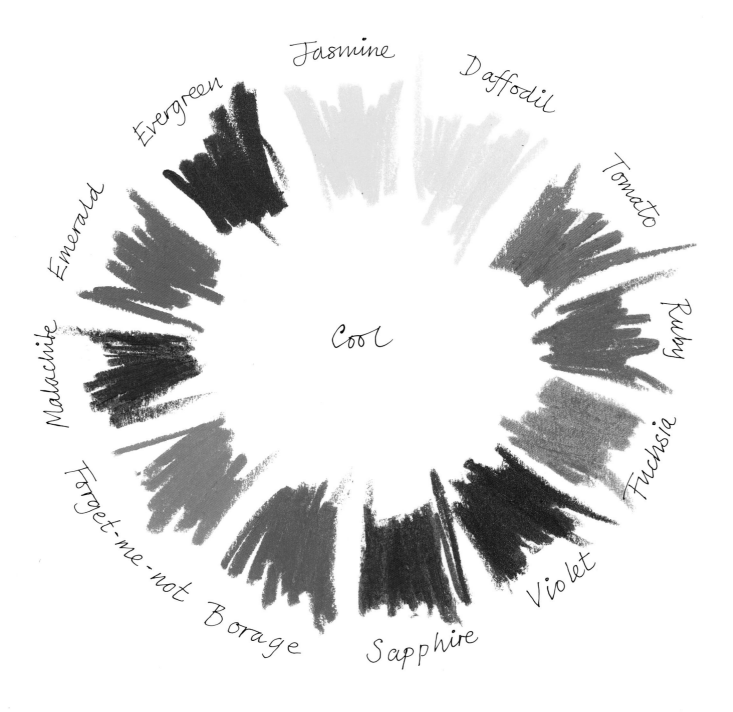

With fire, we come to an element that is bright and vibrant with energy. We often associate fire with destruction, but fire has its quiet aspects too. Think of the glowing embers of a campfire, the gentle warmth of summer evening sun, the blue-white flicker of candlelight. Here is fire that warms and brightens its surroundings.

Still, fire colors in decorating can be hot to handle. More than the other palettes, fire colors must be used carefully and in moderation in order not to overpower the room. However, they can look stunning used as a single color over a large surface area. Colors such as Sunshine and Tourmaline from the warm palette are wonderfully dramatic on the walls. The Ruby, Sapphire and Emerald cool colors make excellent choices for large sofas, curtains and Roman blinds.

Fire colors work beautifully on fabrics that have a natural shine, such as silk and chintz. They can be offset by bold, contemporary floral designs and by intricately patterned carpets and rugs. The fire palette also works well in children's rooms. If you want to make an impact in your home and are drawn to the fire palette, start with a signature color, combined perhaps with a neutral white, and build up the color scheme once you see the effect the main color has in the room.

LEFT The rich fiery reds of the heavy silk curtains combine with the carpet colors to create a bright and dramatic warm color scheme in this sitting room.

RIGHT Cool, pure, bright cobalt walls give a dramatic feel to this compact town kitchen, in keeping with its modern, uncluttered style.

THE
EARTH
PALETTE

THE EARTH PALETTE

The earth palette divides into warm and cool base colors.
Once you have completed the questionnaire on pages
124–25, and have discovered if you are essentially warm-
or cool-based, use the appropriate wheel to select your
colors. These can then be used in decorating or furnishing
your room, either on their own or in combination with
colors from the warm or cool side of the other palettes.

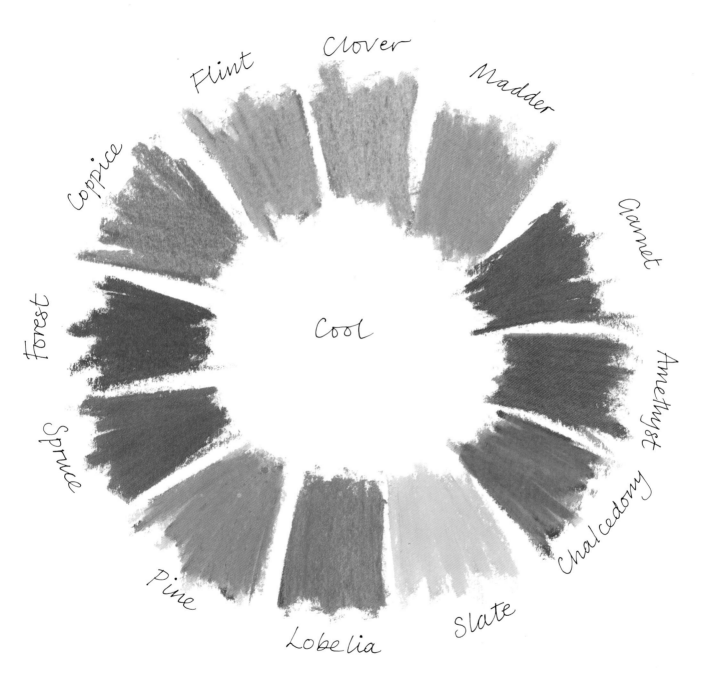

Clover

Flint

Madder

Coppice

Garnet

Forest

Cool

Amethyst

Spruce

Chalcedony

Pine

Slate

Lobelia

Imagine yourself standing on a green carpet, with a yellow wall on your right and a floral wall on your left. Of course, you are not in a room at all, you are in the countryside, with corn ripening on the hill to your right, and a garden on your left. The colors of the earth palette echo those of the natural world, and while the colors of each season may change, the background colors—the colors of the earth—are always present.

The earth palette is both rich and dark, muted and somber. These colors lend themselves most naturally to downstairs rooms, where you want an atmosphere of solid well-being, stability and purpose. They make excellent colors for living rooms, studies and dining rooms, not to mention hallways and corridors. For a dining room, consider using Terracotta or Terraverde from the warm palette; Spruce or Garnet from the cool category. If your rooms receive little natural light, use the richness of the earth palette to enhance them.

The colors of the earth palette work well with dark wood furniture. Mahogany, oak and walnut are particularly effective. Ethnic wooden furnishings from Africa and the Far East are set off to good effect by earth colors, as are large items of wooden furniture such as dining room tables and four-poster beds.

LEFT The bathtub is generally the most important object in any bathroom. Here, its significance is given extra visual emphasis by the contrast between the fiery orange paintwork of the main room and the stark ivory tiles on the walls around the bath. Orange is a difficult color to work with on this scale; here, its possibilities are exploited to the full by a loose dragging in the painting technique. Black and white fittings add a final dramatic flourish.

RIGHT Cool, earthy ochres and dark woodwork accentuate the rustic charm of an unusual oval window in a kitchen.

THE MINERAL PALETTE

THE MINERAL PALETTE

The mineral palette divides into warm and cool base colors.
Once you have completed the questionnaire on pages
124–25, and have discovered if you are essentially warm-
or cool-based, use the appropriate wheel to select your
colors. These can then be used in decorating or furnishing
your room, either on their own or in combination with
colors from the warm or cool side of other palettes.

Obsidian

Bronze

Nutmeg

Nephrite

Tortoiseshell

Angelica

Warm

Copper

Blue John

Rust

Iris

Cinnabar

Elderberry

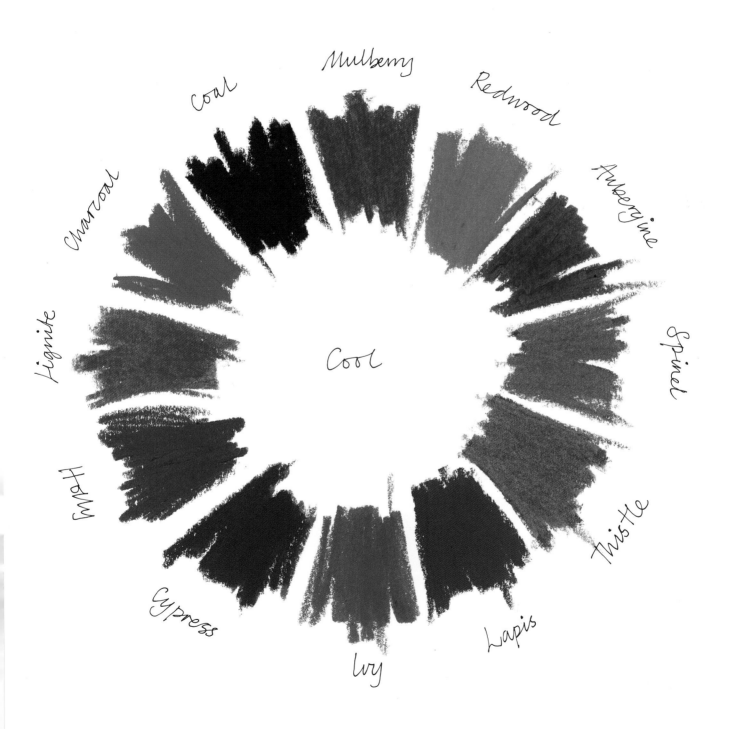

The earth's rich sources of minerals have all been formed by a process of evolution that has taken place millennium after millennium. The resulting colors have an intensity and durability that is timeless. These colors have a more three-dimensional quality than any other palette—rather than looking at a flat surface, you have the impression that you are looking right inside it.

The richness of the mineral palette combines with practical benefits. Here is a range of colors that will wear well without showing every speck of dirt, and will last for years. All the mineral colors make excellent choices for floor-coverings. Choose Nutmeg from the warm side of the pal-

ette or Cedar from the palette's c
stairs, then repeat the color in a s
mum effect. Use reds such as C
rooms where you want a sense of
tion. But do not think that the m
only on a large scale. If you like
make wonderful colors for warm,

As with earth colors, the mine
appropriate for rooms that are u
depth of color works well on rich
trimmings, forming the perfect
entertaining.

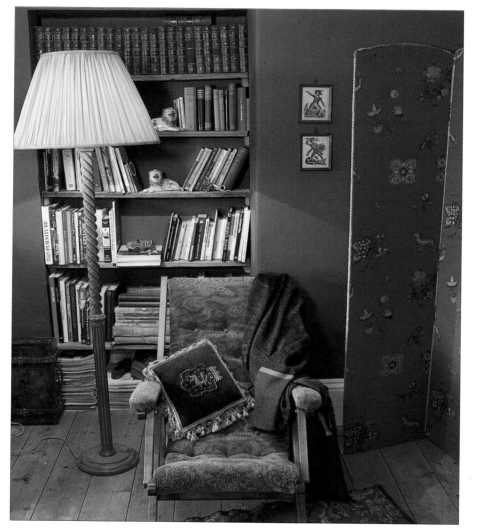

LEFT Against wc
bookshelves an
and lampstand
the screen, the
chair, the Chine
pleats of the lar

RIGHT Cool cor
combine to crec
entrance. The n
the two interior
from each other
and at the same
space between

LIVING WITH COLOR

EVERY BUILDING HAS ITS OWN CHARACTER. WHEN YOU BUY A NEW PROPERTY, OR TAKE A STEP BACK FROM YOUR CURRENT HOME AND CONSIDER CHANGING IT, YOU ARE GIVING YOURSELF THE OPPORTUNITY TO DEVELOP THAT CHARACTER IN A WAY THAT WILL SUIT YOUR OWN REQUIREMENTS. THE NATURAL FEATURES OF A HOME ARE ENHANCED WHEN IT IS DECORATED WITH SENSITIVITY AND CONFIDENCE, GIVING THE PERSONALITY AND TASTE OF THE OWNER ITS FULLEST EXPRESSION. THE MANY EXAMPLES IN THIS SECTION WILL SHOW YOU THE VARIED EFFECTS THAT CAN BE CREATED WITH DIFFERENT COLOR PALETTES AND WILL HELP YOU TO SEE WHAT YOU MIGHT ACHIEVE WITH YOUR OWN COLOR PALETTES.

INTRODUCTION

The inherent character of any home is its primary asset, regardless of scale, age or location. That character may have been concealed for decades or centuries due to clumsy or inappropriate renovation, poor use of available materials and, more often than not, an unimaginative use of color.

BELOW The rustic stonework and curve are left to speak for themselves with the treatment. This natural look continues w of the floor and the wooden furnishings patterned reds, browns and ochers fror a new and appropriately rustic texture. placed mirror reflects and emphasizes

If you have ever looked for a new property, either to rent or to buy, you will recognize the feeling that comes when you find somewhere that, with a new coat of paint here and some carpentry work there, has the potential to be transformed in a way that will reflect your personal taste and style. When you select a new property, the chances are that whatever its condition, you are choosing this place because you can sense that by making a few—or perhaps more than a few—critical changes, you can create a place you will be happy to have as your home.

The room-by-room analysis in this section is intended to help you to identify the chief characteristics of your home, and to develop your own color schemes in order to create a living space in keeping with your taste and your lifestyle. Before looking at rooms on an individual basis, however, it is important that you consider your home as a whole. Even if you plan to decorate only one room, you need to be aware of how your color scheme in that space will influence, and be influenced by, the spaces around it.

One of the most common mistakes made by the inexperienced decorator is creating several different color schemes in neighboring rooms, without taking into account the way in which the different colors will affect each other, and the people who spend time in the rooms. Color always makes an impact, even in the most neutral surroundings. The colors used to decorate a space have an immediate psychological influence on anyone using that space. There may be walls, doors and even stairwells between them, but a succession of rooms in which completely different color palettes have been used will have an unsettling and disjointed effect.

This is not to say that you should not feel free to experiment with color—a house that is decorated in a monotone way, unless it is designed with particular flair, can feel lifeless and dreary—but before you start decorating even a small room, take into account how your plans will relate to the rest of the house.

COLOR AND LIGHT

If you can, give yourself time. Because of the inseparability of color and light, the colors you choose for a room will change according to the time of year, not only because there is more sunlight in the summer months, but also because the quality of light thrown by the sun at different times of year can alter the character of a room quite drastically. This is particularly true of west-facing rooms, where the windows will be dark by late afternoon in winter but flooded by sunshine well into the evening during the summer months. The same differences apply to the morning light in east-facing rooms, though they will probably be less relevant unless you are a very early riser. North- and south-facing rooms will not change to the same extent at different times of year, but you will need to consider whether the natural light is going to be blocked by nearby buildings or by overhanging trees, especially when the sun is low in winter.

Pay attention to detail when you are planning a color scheme. Imagine the room like a jigsaw puzzle where all the pieces have to fit together. It is surprising how easily a well coordinated room can be thrown out of balance. Even a detail as small as a picture frame of the wrong color can ruin the appearance of an otherwise harmonious color scheme. So can a badly placed lamp, or an inappropriate lampshade—red lampshades, for example, throw a pink cast unless they have a white or ivory lining. Even a vase of flowers can spoil a room if the colors are not in keeping with their surroundings.

Last but not least, enjoy yourself. Experiment. When you are looking for inspiration, do not be afraid to ask for as many samples as you like. Daub test paint on the wall and pin up wallpaper and fabric samples alongside. Visit the room off and on over a period of time, noting the difference evident in the color samples seen in daylight versus artificial light. Be adventurous. Remember that once you have decided on your color palette, you have a completely sound base from which to transform your home. You don't need to make expensive mistakes, and if you make the occasional cheap one, you should regard it as part of a natural learning process, not as a sign that you don't know what you are doing.

Successful color styling turns around a few elementary rules. Once you have mastered them, the floor, the ceiling and everything in between are yours.

DESIGNING YOUR HOME

Even if they are the same size and shape and built out of the same materials, no two houses have ever been alike, for the simple reason that they cannot both share the same plot of ground—and the setting of a house plays a major part in its character. So your starting point in color styling your home is to consider its setting.

THE HOUSE AS A UNIT

Be aware of the expectations your house awakens in you as you approach it, then consider how you can best realize those expectations. Are there any features outside the house that you want to continue to develop inside it? For exam-

ple, if your home is in a rural setting, is this a theme you want to continue indoors? If you live in a city, are there historical aspects of the city as a whole, and your neighborhood in particular, that you would like to echo inside? Or do you want to achieve a complete change of environment as you step across the threshold?

A SIGNATURE COLOR

Color can extend walls, raise and lower ceilings, eliminate corners. It can make the same space airy or womb-like, formal or intimate, stimulating or peaceful. To achieve a sense of continuity and openness, use the same color for the walls and carpets of successive rooms. To achieve a sense of distance and separation, choose contrasting colors. You may like to combine these options in different areas of your home. For example, you may want your living room and hall to connect visually, and then to have a contrast between the living room and the kitchen.

LEFT The chief architectural features of this bedroom are the wooden paneled ceiling, the handsome fireplace and the windows on either side. This room receives plenty of natural light, a feature the owner has developed by choosing pale whites and ivories to establish the signature color. Additional interest is achieved by the use of contrasting textures on the carpet, armchairs and curtains, and by introducing dark color accents with the bed frame, curtain poles, mirror frame, candlesticks, lampstand and chair.

ABOVE In this kitchen earth colors are combined with accents from the water palette. Handsome blue-green cupboards provide the storage space and the foreground color. A pale wooden work surface divides the upper and lower units and at the same time picks up the mellow apricot-pink of the walls. This warm base color in turn offsets the display of blue and white china.

However you plan your overall scheme, establish a signature color. One of the simplest ways of establishing this connection is by having the same floor surface running throughout the house. But this is not the only way of creating a sense of unity—you may choose to have the color of the wall paint in your entrance hall echoed in one of the colors in a patterned living room carpet, for example, or in the curtains of a bedroom. When you select a signature color and make sure it is used, however minimally, as a connecting thread running through your house, your overall color scheme will cohere in a way that is both visually and psychologically satisfying.

When a house has distinctive features, it is better to emphasize than to ignore them. If you try to play them down, you run the risk of the house disappearing into its own borders. Strong features call for strong definition. If you house has architectural features such as exposed beams, unusually proportioned rooms, interesting alcoves or detailed woodwork, play up the benefits of these features. With wood paneling, echo the feature of the panels by painting recessed surfaces darker than relief ones. Paint the interiors of cupboards and the backs of shelving a shade darker than the walls to emphasize their depth.

Although it sounds too obvious to require attention, be aware of whom, besides yourself, your home is intended for. If you have a partner whose taste does not entirely accord with your own, resolve your differences if you can by allocating him or her one room and giving yourself another. Avoid the kind of compromise by which one person chooses the carpet and the other the wallpaper. If you have small children, you will need to pay attention to the wear-and-tear factor and choose flooring and wall treatments that will withstand the thundering of small feet and the patina of sticky fingers. And if you share a house with teenagers, make sure you leave them enough space for their own particular kind of self-expression.

Be conscious of your budget as you work out your color scheme. A few cans of paint can go further in transforming a home than a week's worth of carpentry. Give yourself time to be a sleuth and check out different manufacturers' prices. Don't be afraid to negotiate a discount, especially if you are buying large quantities of fabric or flooring. Besides considering the expense of the materials themselves, consider the cost in time that will be devoted to decorating. Decide too just how much time you have to spend in maintaining your home. For example, if you like the idea of filling a window frame with rows of colored glass vases that will sparkle like gems in the light, consider how often they will have to be cleaned. Some colors show the dirt much more easily than others; avoid black tiles in the bathroom and kitchen if you want to have a low-maintenance home.

PLANNING AHEAD

First work out your priorities. If you need to do some rewiring to achieve the lighting effects you want, think ahead and make sure the electrical work is carried out before you start decorating. Check for dampness and dry rot too and ensure that window and door frames and baseboards are in good condition before you strip and repaint them. It is more economical in the long run to attend to these basic areas of maintenance before you embark on a decorating program.

If you are the kind of person who enjoys variety and likes to alter your surroundings on quite a regular basis, introduce elements that can be inexpensively altered for a different effect. Rugs, lampshades, cushions and cotton throws in a sitting room; towels and soaps in a bathroom; new biscuit tins, place mats and chair covers in a kitchen can all ring in color changes with minimal financial outlay.

THE THREE COLOR KEYS

All the colors contained within a living space play a part in creating the character of that space. But, as a basic rule, the colors in a room can be subdivided into the following three areas:

Base colors
Foreground colors
Color accents

Each of these color keys has an essential role. And the relationship in both color and tone between the different color keys is as important as the contribution made by them individually.

BASE COLORS All shades of color have a base "note." With primary colors, that note is inseparable from the color itself—primary red does not have any other color added to it, nor does primary blue or yellow. However, the majority of paints, wallpapers and furnishing fabrics on the market all contain secondary or tertiary colors, in an almost infinite variety of tints and shades. The base note of a tertiary color can differ from the "apparent" surface color. For example, a light beige with a blue base will give a different effect from a light beige with a yellow base.

As discussed in the first chapter, all colors have either a warm base or a cool base. When choosing your colors, you need, first, to be clear about which you are selecting. The difference between a warm green and a cool green may appear to be slight on a paint chart or a fabric sample, but when that color is used across an extensive surface in a room, the base color in the paint will have a significant influence on the result. Your base color is not only the base note of the paint, wallpaper or fabric you have chosen, it is

also the basis of your overall color scheme. In some cases the base color of a room is already apparent. If, for example, you have a wooden floor that you do not wish to cover, that will establish the base color for the room and you need to choose a wall color that complements the wood.

The base colors of any space are the colors that occupy the widest areas—usually the walls, the floor and the ceiling. Because the impact of a color increases in direct proportion to the expanse it covers, the quality of the base color has an overriding influence on the character of a room.

FOREGROUND COLORS Foreground colors are those that dominate in the furnishings of a room. They can include the colors in sofas, tables, chairs, beds, mantelpieces, alcoves and shelving, floor rugs, curtains and blinds. Foreground colors need to harmonize with the base colors, which means that your base color needs to be either present or suggested in your foreground colors. The only exception to this is if you are intentionally creating a dramatic effect, which is achieved by combining strongly contrasting base and foreground colors.

If your foreground colors are mixed, as in a multi-colored sofa or a patterned set of curtains, you have the opportunity to select a base color that will emphasize one of the colors in your furnishing scheme. For example, a patterned curtain fabric that contains some pink will look pinker if the walls are painted pink than if they are painted pale gray. Conversely, you may choose to work with more than one base color, such as by using a striped wallpaper. In this case, you may opt to select a foreground color that strengthens the presence in the room of one or another of the colors used in the design of the wallpaper.

ABOVE LEFT The fire palette plays a dominant role as the foreground color in this sitting room. Strong, geometric patterns on the central rug and in the curtains link these two features and introduce a wide range of colors. The red trim of the chairs accentuates this color and contrasts strongly both with the dark green fabric and with the pale walls and window frame behind.

ABOVE The textures of both plain and painted wood, paintwork, glazed cups and saucers, eggs, fruit and flowers all play a part in making the color scheme of this kitchen interesting as well as harmonious.

COLOR ACCENTS Color accents are colors that are introduced to enliven the overall color scheme of a room. Color accents may be introduced through cushions, stencil patterns, wall friezes and dado rails, baseboards, piping on soft furnishings, picture and photograph mounts and frames, lamp bases and lampshades, found objects, wall hangings and table settings. Because the interplay between complementary colors is livelier than that between harmonious or matching colors, color accents are often complementary to the base color in a room. Thus, red accents will introduce energy and warmth to a green room, while purple accents will glamorize a yellow-based room. However, the neutrals can also perform well as accents—a few charcoal-gray accents will introduce sophistication in a yellow color scheme and soften the impact of a predominantly red room. White as a color accent can throw into sharper relief many rich and dark shades, while dark brown and black can give definition and strength to pale, off-white color schemes.

THE INFLUENCE OF TEXTURE

Chintz, linen, calico. Wool, seagrass, slate. Pine, walnut, formica. All of these different textures, and more, contribute to the effect colors have on a room. This is due in part to the varying ways in which light plays off objects of different textures, and in part to the way placing different textures alongside one another has a tactile as well as a visual impact on a room. Combining a wide variety of textures is one of the best ways of bringing interest to a monochrome decorating scheme. Conversely, combining as few textures as possible can increase the sense of space and introduce a note of restrained elegance to a color scheme.

WOOD When it is unvarnished, wood has a matt surface that will absorb light rather than reflect it, resulting in a restful, rustic atmosphere. Unvarnished wood can be a marvelous starting point for a color scheme—like any natural material, wood contains a myriad of subtly different shades and colors that alter from hour to hour with changes of light.

Because of its shiny surface, varnished wood reflects light. This makes it a stylish and dramatic choice for rooms that will be used for entertaining in the evening. The play of candlelight or electric light on highly varnished wood creates an atmosphere of sparkling elegance, which is emphasized by the contrast between the solidity of the wood and the floating, translucent quality of the light. The interplay between wood and light is further

enhanced by the use of a dark base color—this applies to both unvarnished and varnished wooden surfaces. The mid-blues make particularly comfortable companions to wood, as do the blue-greens, while the mid-reds create a more energetic mood.

GLASS Glass is an excellent way of enhancing light and accentuating color in a room. Before the advent of electricity, this consideration was a salient factor in the choice of crystal and colored glass for chandeliers. Glass objects are

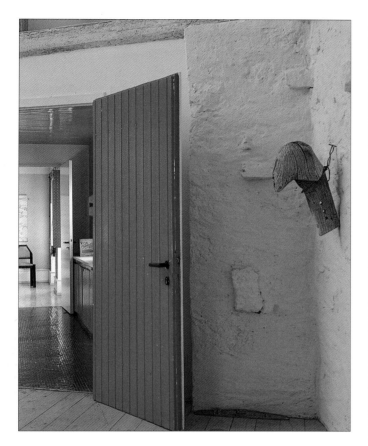

ABOVE The wooden door of this hall is given special importance by being painted bright red, which sets it off from everything around it and underlines its significance as an entrance.

LEFT Against a stark white background, a rich and subtle combination of tiles from the mineral palette provides the foreground color in this shower room. Brightly colored towels are all that is needed to provide color accents.

best positioned where they can catch light and extend it; they are wasted in recesses and shadowy corners. All kinds of glass objects—clear, colored or opaque—will introduce a note of richness and brightness to a room. Clear glass will also pick up the colors around it, while colored glass can be used as a color accent that will seem to float against the surfaces behind it. Judiciously placed mirrors are also valuable allies in planning a color scheme, as they can reflect another room and prepare one for a change of color in moving to another setting.

DECORATING DO'S AND DON'TS

DO

✔ Make structural changes, such as rewiring, reflooring or building shelves, before you start to decorate

✔ Establish a budget

✔ Consider the function of each room in turn, including:
- the time of day it will be used
- how many people are likely to use it at any given time
- the amount of wear and tear it will receive
- the amount of time you can commit to maintaining it
- its location in relation to the rest of the house
- its light sources, both natural and artificial
- storage

✔ Select a signature color

✔ Be aware that the colors of one room will affect those of the rooms around it

✔ Note all architectural details

✔ Experiment with sample boards

✔ Take into account the needs and tastes of family or house mates

DON'T

✘ Buy the first fabric or paint you like without researching the market

✘ Mix and match colors before you have compared them as samples

✘ Make guesses; instead, measure, compare and consider before you buy

✘ Be impractical—you will probably regret a white carpet

✘ Ignore details

✘ Hurry; you should introduce your new color elements stage by stage

✘ Take short cuts

✘ Combine colors from different palettes unless you are intentionally creating a specific effect

✘ Use lots of black and purple

✘ Paint over valuable wooden furniture; sell the piece and buy cheaper wood if you want to use paint

MAKING A SAMPLE BOARD

Professional interior designers use sample boards as a way of experimenting with possible combinations of color, texture and style. The sample board enables you to see in miniature how well different colors, fabrics and patterns look alongside each other. It also gives you a cheap, easy and enjoyable way of adding and subtracting different elements to your room design. To swap one fabric for another on a sample board will cost you next to nothing; to have another complete set of curtains made because your first choice did not work out is not only expensive, it also undermines your confidence and stops you giving your sense of color its fullest expression.

So, make the preparation of sample boards a priority for every room you plan to decorate. Photocopy the checklist on this page as many times as you need and take it with you when you go shopping. Then follow the four easy steps listed opposite. Even if you know it will take you two or three years to buy everything you want in your new room, do not be afraid to include all the items on the sample board. The clearer your vision is at the start, the more complete your room will look at the finish. And simply by arranging and rearranging the ingredients of the sample board, you will learn more about color, and also about your own stylistic preferences, than you will by searching through sample after sample in a soft furnishings store.

CHECKLIST

SIZE
❍ How big is your room?
❍ width......................
❍ length....................
❍ height.....................

COLOR
❍ Which existing colors do you wish to retain? Which new colors do you wish to introduce?
- floor
- ceiling
- carpet/rug
- woodwork
- curtains
- soft furnishings
- walls
- furniture
- accessories
- pictures
- lampshades and stands

LIGHT
❍ How much natural light does the room receive, and at what time of day?
❍ What kind of artificial light do you wish to use?
- overhead
- standard lamps
- uplighters
- candles

Use different shades of a color from sample paint charts—build up your color palette with different cards.

A photogra of a room i your last home acts a reminder the furnishin you have.

Use photographs from magazines to illustrate different curtain styles.

Include individual paint colors for specific projects.

Photographs of the room as it is now act as a reminder of what has to be done and what is in the room.

Have a large sample of the main fabric to use as a base for the other items.

Take photographs of rugs to help you color-coordinate fabrics and other furnishings.

Build up a collection of coordinating fabrics that can be used for cushions and general color accents.

Try out a large sample of fabric to see if the scale suits the piece of furniture.

STEP 1

Buy a piece of foam board 16 x 24in (40cm x 60cm) and a pack of thumb tacks at your local art supplier. Assemble on the board samples of all the items in the room, such as furnishing fabric, that you wish to keep as they are. Take photographs of any large items such rugs, lamps, pictures or main pieces of furniture so these can be included on the sample board in some way.

STEP 2

Add samples, such as pieces of carpet or paint manufacturer's color charts, for each of the base colors you are considering.

STEP 3

Now add samples of, for example, curtain or upholstery fabric for all the foreground colors you are considering using.

STEP 4

Finally, add samples of coordinating colors and color accents, in the form of fabric for cushion covers or throws, tablecloths or lampshades.

Do not regard each of these stages as rigid. The purpose of making a sample board is to enable you to go to and fro, adding and subtracting different base, foreground and accent colors, to get a sense of how the room will work as a unit once it is finished. Move the different samples around on the board so that you can see how the atmosphere of your room may change, depending on which colors are placed alongside one another. With the sample board in the room you intend to decorate, see how the colors you have selected change at different times of day.

THE ENTRANCE HALL

Your entrance hall gives you your first opportunity to say, "this is who I am." You may want to make this statement discreet, playful or dramatic.

Whatever your inclination, the way in which you decorate the entrance hall will be the first indication to visitors of your taste and lifestyle and the way in which you are likely to have planned the rest of your home. Your entrance hall will show, among other things, how seriously you take yourself; how strong your sense of color is; how effectively you are able to introduce yourself to others. Even when they amount to a space no larger than a corridor, entrances speak—and because they have the first say, it is worth taking them seriously.

THE FRONT DOOR

The entrance hall starts with the front door, and the walls on either side of it. To what extent do you want the characteristics that lie outside your home to be extended indoors? If you are lucky enough to live in a beautiful rural location, you may opt to emphasize the character of the local materials by painting the walls of the entrance hall in a hue that echoes that of the outer stonework, or the colors of the countryside. Similarly, if you have a brick house, you may wish to carry indoors the natural warmth that much brickwork contains. On the other hand, if you feel that the exterior of your home lacks character, or if you want to introduce a different character to that which is outside, here is the place to establish your personal identity.

PROPORTIONS AND WAYS WITH WALL SPACE

Consider the proportions of the space you have to work with. If your hall is tall and narrow, and you want to break up the walls, it is worth considering a dado rail, with the area below the rail painted a solid color and the area above wallpapered or painted a lighter shade. As well as being an

RIGHT The color of natural wood combines with a warm green from the earth palette in this spacious hallway—a wise choice in a space that receives little natural light.

❍ The tiled floor coordinates with the warm wood of the staircase and doorway.

❍ Wooden bookshelves around the far door frame make a distinctive feature out of a wall area that would otherwise be inconspicuous.

❍ The wood and fabric of the director's chair pick up the two main colors of the room.

❍ The theme of wood is continued in the coat rack, which also makes good use of what would otherwise be wasted space.

❍ Four overhead spotlights focus discreetly but effectively on the center of the room.

RIGHT Three harmonizing paint colors from the water palette bring elegance as well as light to this simple stairwell. Note that the back of the alcove on the left is painted the same soft mauve as the stairwell, accentuating the light green wall and taking the eye upstairs. The airy wall colors are beautifully offset by the golden sheen of the varnished wooden floor.

FAR RIGHT Here the dado rail gives architectural balance to a narrow, paneled hallway, set off by the unusual random mix of different-colored floor tiles.

effective way of dividing vertical space, a dado rail also gives you the opportunity to use a practical color for the lower wall surfaces, which are likely to receive the most wear and tear. Alternatively, you may have a hallway that is large enough to be treated as a reception room. In much earlier times, halls were often multifunctional, containing a large fireplace as a focal point and intended to be used both for relaxation and eating. Large entrance halls also characterize many Georgian and Edwardian houses. If your entrance hall offers the kind of space that can accommodate a sitting area, a desk by a window or a child's rocking horse, you will be able to plan your color scheme around these objects and create an ambience that tempts the visitor to stop and linger for a while.

Do not be deceived into thinking that a narrow entrance hall, with space for no more than a hat stand, has to be boring. As advertisers know well, people enjoy being diverted as they move from one place to another—witness the number of advertisements on roadsides and in subway stations. An entrance hall can make a most effective picture gallery, even if space is at a premium. You do not need to be an art connoisseur or to spend a lot of money to hang a row of pictures, prints or photographs in your hallway.

Hanging pictures

If you do choose to hang pictures in an entrance hall, you need to be conscious of lighting. It is no use having a fascinating arrangement of prints if no one can see them properly. If you choose overhead lighting, you need to make sure that the fittings you choose throw sufficient light to do justice to all of your picture collection. You may also consider having a discreet tube of light running below a picture rail, or a pair of strategically placed uplighters. Many entrance halls, particularly in apartments and town houses, do not have a source of natural light from windows so it is worth taking time and trouble over lighting this part of your home well. Nothing is less inviting than stepping into a poorly lit entrance hall.

Bear in mind that many pictures are enhanced by being hung against a dark color. Black-and-white prints can look dramatic against deep blues, greens and reds, as can old

family photographs. Yellow makes a better background for works of art that contain a lot of color—its brightness can overpower sepia or black-and-white images.

Matting plays an important part in the overall effect of a display of pictures. It may seem to be a small detail, but pictures that have an ivory mat will look different from those with a cream or a light blue mat. Similarly, gilt frames will introduce a different accent to plain wood or lacquer frames. Pictures can also be decorated with ribbons and bows. Pay attention not only to the images you choose, but the way in which you mat, frame and hang them.

Special paint effects

If you prefer to make the walls a feature in their own right, you might consider using a patterned wallpaper, or a special paint effect such as *trompe l'oeil*. Because the entrance hall is the crossover place between the outer and inner worlds, it is an ideal space in which to paint imitation brickwork or stonework. A hallway can also be enhanced by having a stenciled frieze or a stenciled dado rail.

FLOORING

Flooring is of primary importance in entrance halls. This is the place where mud, rain and slush will be brought inside during wintery weather, where umbrellas will drip on the floor and where rain will run from overcoats. One way to remind people that they are no longer outside is to devote several feet of your entrance hall to coarse matting that is specifically intended for vigorous shoe- and boot-rubbing. If you do not have the space or the inclination for this, make sure that you have a decent doormat and that the flooring of the rest of the entrance hall is hardwearing, easy to clean and of a shade that does not make every speck of dirt shine out like a beacon.

CONNECTING ROOMS WITH COLOR

More often than not, entrance halls connect to several rooms, so however you decorate the hallway, you need to ensure a smooth transition from this part of the home to the rooms that lead off it. You don't need to repeat every color in your hall in all of the neighboring rooms, but you should not change absolutely everything either. As discussed earlier in this section, establish your signature color and pick it up again, either as a base or a foreground color, in the adjacent living spaces.

STAIRWELLS

If you are laying a new carpet on the stairs, you can choose whether to run the carpet right across the stair width or leave a border of white or natural woodwork on either side of the carpet. In a house with one or more upper landings, you can introduce a subtle change of atmosphere on each floor. For example, you may paint the walls of the ground floor in a warm off-white, then enrich this on the next floor with a warm cream and brighten it on the upper floor with a stronger yellow. Or you may select a dark, assertive green on the ground floor, changing to a patterned paper on the next floor in which the same green is a secondary color, and taking the primary color of the wallpaper as your theme for the upper floor. Whatever you decide, aim to achieve an effect that makes your entrance hall interesting in its own right and a space that invites the visitor to explore further.

Many town houses have narrow hallways that can feel tunnel-like and that have nowhere to place a piece of furniture. By introducing a dado rail, placing a shelf above the radiator and continuing the dado molding around the shelf, you create a useful display and storage space while maintaining a unified look. Adding a mirror above the dado rail gives a feeling of width and space and sets off the display of prints to advantage.

YOU WILL NEED:

○ Length of wooden dado molding, approximately 2in (5cm) deep, to go around the mirror and the shelf

○ Length of wood for shelf, approximately 7in (17cm) deep and ⅝in (1.5cm) thick. For the length, measure that of the radiator itself and add 8–12in (20–30cm) to allow space on either side to fix brackets.

○ A pair of shelf brackets and 2in (50mm) screws for fixing

○ Carpenter's level

○ Mirror glass cut to size and 4 flat mirror screws for hanging

○ Narrow wooden beading as long as the width of the mirror

CREATING SPACE IN A NARROW HALL

1. Buy the mirror glass with a hole drilled at each corner and screw it to the wall, centered above the radiator, using the flat screws. Fix the dado rail along the hall walls, stopping 4–6in (10–15cm) from the radiator, at each side.

2. Screw the first bracket in position, using a wall plug in a solid wall, then use a shelf and the level to position the second bracket and fix it in the same way.

3. Place the shelf in position above the radiator, using the level to align the ends before fixing them securely to the brackets. Continue the dado molding around the shelf, mitering the corners; use headless nails to fix it in place. Fix dado molding around three sides of the mirror, using wood glue. Finish by applying the narrow wooden beading to cover the base of the mirror.

CAROLYN'S TIPS

❝ By painting the mirror frame and dado rail a pale color, you will enhance the feeling of space and light in the hall. ❞

❝ To lower a high ceiling, paint the dado rail a darker color. ❞

❝ Create color accents by painting the mirror frame in a contrasting color. ❞

THE LIVING ROOM

In any home the living room calls for special attention since it is the room in which the family will spend time together and visitors will be entertained.

Planning a color scheme for a living room means creating a space in which everyone can quickly feel at their ease and ready to socialize. At their worst, living rooms are cold and inhospitable, making it difficult to relax. At their best, they are warm, inviting and so comfortable that you find it difficult to leave them.

COLOR AND COMFORT

Color and comfort are key factors in the creation of a successful living room. These two themes come together in the choices you make for the upholstery of your armchairs and sofas, since these are likely to make up the most dominant foreground colors in the room. Solid colors are often a popular choice, and if you follow this route you can introduce a variety of patterns and textures with throw pillows and cotton throws. Alternatively, you may opt to reverse this process and choose a multicolored upholstery fabric, highlighting a particular color within it by using plain cushions.

Color and comfort are also the key themes in creating a living room that is as welcoming to one person as it is to many. For most of us, the living room is a multifunctional space. You will probably want to feel as settled in it when you are alone as you do when you are hosting a party or having your sister and her children to tea. It is horrible to sit in a room and feel you are surrounded by empty spaces. A simple way of resolving this problem is by varying the upholstery you choose for different sofas and armchairs. Not only does this break up the space visually, it also has the psychological benefit of separating different items of furniture so that their presence is not overbearing to the solitary occupant.

RIGHT Powerful reds from the mineral palette give an inviting and almost oriental character to this sitting room.

❍ The bold, star-patterned wallpaper is beautifully offset by the blue marbled paintwork below the dado rail.

❍ Two wall bracket lights balance the gold-framed Indian cushion covers that are treated as pictures, while the lamps on either side of the sofa create a pleasing contrast of color and scale.

❍ White-painted woodwork separates the dark colors from each other and lightens the room's overall effect. At the same time it accentuates the contrast between the red wallpaper and sofa and the blue paint below the dado.

❍ The red sofa repeats the signature color of the room, and the richly patterned array of cushions unites all the colors.

LEFT The exposed wooden beams are a distinctive feature of this country sitting room. The natural theme continues in the carpet and the background color on the walls and is picked up in all the soft furnishings.

RIGHT Simple base colors from the natural palette provide the perfect foil for a range of decorative items from the earth palette, including the display of pottery and books on the shelves and the magnificent textile on the right-hand wall.

CHOOSING A SIGNATURE COLOR

As in any room, your choice of signature color will affect the atmosphere created. If you want a feeling of warmth and intimacy, a rich base color can be a good choice because the walls will darken during the evening and contrast strongly with the areas of light in the room. This atmosphere can be heightened by choosing a heavy curtain fabric, so that the room feels well wrapped, especially on cold winter nights.

LIVING WITH RED

Inevitably, reds are popular as living room colors because they have a warming and stimulating effect, making them a distinct asset in a social setting. However, bear in mind that red makes objects look larger than they really are. For this reason, red can benefit from being combined with large areas of natural colors, particularly in a small space. If used as background colors on walls, the darker reds need spacious rooms to perform effectively. Used in excess, the drama of red can become darkly claustrophobic. So if you have a red carpet, balance its impact by choosing naturals or light tints for your walls. Conversely, red walls need to be balanced by a more muted floor treatment, though they also look well with the rich patterns of oriental carpets, in which the mix of many deep colors will "anchor" the red of the walls.

RIGHT Two shades of green, a sage green on the sofa and a blue-green on the walls, establish water as the dominant palette of this sitting room. A rich paisley carpet, heavy wooden furnishings, crowded bookshelves and dark oil paintings create an air of studiousness and privacy.

LIVING WITH YELLOW

Yellows are often chosen for living rooms, particularly in cooler climates. The paler yellows create a sophisticated, elegant atmosphere while the brighter ones can make a large reception room appear more inviting and a small one more luminous and spacious. All the yellows are beautifully complemented by grays, mid-blues and purples, and different shades of yellow can be combined with excellent results—a strong yellow on the walls can be off-set by floral or abstract fabric for curtains and cushions that contain a predominance of creamier yellows and mid-blues. Think of yellow as an accent color for darker color schemes.

LIVING WITH BEIGES AND NATURALS

Although it can be dreary when it is used without awareness of its qualities, beige can be an excellent background color for a living room. Beige is a chameleon, strongly affected by its companion colors. When you choose a beige, be aware of its base color: a pink beige will emphasize reds while a yellow beige will relieve them; a blue beige will complement yellow furnishings while a yellow beige complements green.

The components of many successful color schemes, naturals can come into their own in living rooms. If you want a room that feels spacious and harmonious, choose a scheme that is predominantly natural, with variety introduced

RIGHT Light-toned natural background colors are punctuated by dark mineral colors in this airy sitting room. The finest of blinds and the white walls take full advantage of the natural light and at the same time create a neutral backdrop for a variety of interesting objects. The handsome marble fireplace is highlighted by hanging a picture above it and placing a hand-crafted vase to one side of the mantelpiece. Black fabric on the chair covers and deep purple cushions provide bold foreground colors and ensure that the overall effect is not too bland.

ABOVE A wide range of carefully chosen colors and textures from the wind palette combine to give this room its charm. The rich reds of the rug make it the centerpiece of the room. This role is emphasized by containing the use of red—repeated only in the tapestry stool. The natural tones are taken up as the signature color for the hand-painted paneled walls and soft furnishings.

Stylish window treatments do not have to be expensive. The simplest brown-and-white gingham has been used for these curtains, their tiny check pattern creating a subtle and pleasing contrast to the plain walls and floral chintzes. Two cushions on the sofa echo the gingham of the curtains, while another two use the same fabric as the cloths on the occasional tables to the left and right of the window. Parchment shades on the lamp cast a warm and mellow light, creating a perfect atmosphere for evening relaxation or entertaining.

through the use of different textures. A few dark accents, particularly dark woods, will enrich a natural color scheme and create a serene and restful atmosphere.

THE FIREPLACE AS A FOCAL POINT

The focal point of many living rooms is the fireplace. This is often the feature around which the design of the room will turn, particularly if it boasts a distinctive mantelpiece. It may well be the first feature to be seen when entering a room. If your living room has a handsome fireplace, you may regard it as the main source of energy in the room. So the way in which you "dress" the fireplace makes a significant statement.

A fireplace can be emphasized by hanging a mirror or a particularly striking picture above it; by running bookshelves or display shelves the full length of the wall on either side of it; and by choosing a fireside rug that complements any colors in the mantelpiece. Other simple and more temporary ways of emphasizing your fireplace include arranging ornaments of a particular type, such as colored glass, wooden objects or a collection of candlesticks on the mantelpiece; or using the space for a display of miniature books, lacquer boxes or photographs.

LIGHTING

Lighting plays a major part in creating a welcoming atmosphere. Overhead lighting can be severe in living rooms, particularly if the light fitting hangs from the center of the ceiling. A bright overhead light can easily eclipse other elements in a room, whereas wall brackets, standard lamps and uplighters can be used in combination to emphasize particular features. For a bright atmosphere, combine table lamps with wall lighting, then turn the wall lights down to create a more intimate and informal ambience.

RINGING THE CHANGES

Above all, living rooms are to be enjoyed all year round. Once you have established your color scheme and installed your main furniture, you are free to experiment—with lighting, with flowers, with rugs, with pictures, with cushions, with shelving. You will be surprised by how many simple ways there are of changing and enhancing the mood of the room according to the season.

CREATE AN INSTANT LIBRARY

What was once a fireplace has been skillfully converted into useful storage space with a *trompe l'oeil* bookshelf above. A mixture of shades from the wind palette have been combined to make the book spines, creating a distinctive feature out of an awkward space.

YOU WILL NEED:

❍ Wooden doweling in three different widths, ½in–1½in (1–4cm) wide, to imitate book spines (offcuts can often be bought more cheaply)

❍ Wooden battens ⅜in–⅝in (1.5cm–2cm) wide to make the fake shelves

❍ Wooden dado molding to surround the bookcase

❍ Wood glue

❍ Matt, eggshell and/or satin-finish paint in appropriate colors for the shelf fronts, moldings, background and book spines

❍ Plumb line, steel rule and pencil

1. Mark out the bookcase area, using the plumb line, steel rule and pencil, and paint it dark gray or another dark color. Mark straight horizontal lines on the wall, approximately 10in (25cm) apart, using the steel rule and pencil, then glue the fake shelves in place, leaving space between them for the book spines. Apply the dado molding around the outside edge, using wood glue. Paint the shelf fronts and dado molding to match the other woodwork in the room.

2. Cut the wooden doweling into lengths approximately 9–10in (23–25cm) long, varying them slightly, to make the book spines, and paint them in different colors. Leave to dry. Using wood glue, stick the wooden strips in place, varying their sizes, colors and positions, to give the random effect of books stored in a bookcase.

CAROLYN'S TIPS

❝ By varying the length and widths of the wooden doweling, you will create a more realistic "library" effect. It is a good idea to place some at a slight angle to imitate the appearance of real books leaning against others on a shelf. I have made the lengths of doweling on the top shelf consistently shorter (approximately 7in/18cm) to give the effect of a row of paperback books. ❞

❝ I have painted the book spines a mixture of shades from the wind palette to make an original and eye-catching feature out of what was formerly an awkward space. ❞

INSPIRATION: If you wish, write witty book titles on the wooden spines.

THE DINING ROOM

Eating together, however informally, is one of the few rituals still practiced on a daily basis in households the world over.

In a dining room, the central grouping of a table and chairs at which people will come together to share meals instantly creates an air of formality. Whether the meal is a light brunch, a children's gathering or an elaborate dinner party, there is a quality of order, discipline and definition about a table that has been carefully laid for a meal—and the challenge to the interior designer is to bring warmth and character to this setting.

Luckily, this challenge contains its own opportunities. The very fact that dining rooms are used at varying times of day for different types of meal provides scope for creating a room that changes according to the occasion. You may want to reserve your dining room for entertaining only, but if you want a space where you can also spread out your sewing things on the table, let your children sit and do their homework or serve breakfast for six or supper for two, you need to create a setting that is both welcoming and versatile.

THE TABLE AS A FOCAL POINT

The focal point of any dining room is the table and here you can introduce changes cheaply and simply for different occasions. A bright, vinyl-coated tablecloth will protect your tabletop against the activities of preschool children; crisp white damask, still popular after hundreds of years, is hard to beat for a formal lunch or dinner party, while gingham, paisley and floral tablecloths make excellent backdrops for informal lunches and family meals. You may like to create a layered look by combining a plain, floor-length tablecloth with a shorter, patterned one laid on top of it. This looks particularly effective with round tables, and is an economical way of creating a stylish look without needing to invest in a high-quality table. You can also introduce different colors through tablemats, napkins, coasters, colored glass

RIGHT A wide range of colors from the earth palette have been brought together in this unusual dining room. The creator of the room has made the most of every inch of space, using images of fruit that make it mouth-watering simply to cross the threshold. This is everything that a dining room should be.

❍ Dark, polished floorboards are left bare, anchoring the plain wooden table and matching benches.

❍ A single curtain of heavy, richly patterned fabric hangs in an extravagant swag, at the same time admitting more light from outside than would be allowed by a pair of curtains. The curtain is hung with an almost theatrical precision, setting the stage for drinks and coffee in the garden beyond.

❍ Warm yellow walls create a fresh, inviting atmosphere and offset a rich range of prints, each displaying a different fruit.

❍ On the table, glassware sparkles in the light, a theme that is discreetly echoed in the lamps on either side of the French windows. Black lampshades both contain and enhance their separate pools of light.

RIGHT Against a pale window treatment from the natural palette, a simple yet charming combination of blues and yellows from the air palette gives this dining table a distinctive feminine note. The round table is an important factor in the overall effect, avoiding the need for any sharp angles, and blowsy pink and white tulips create an eye-catching centerpiece.

beakers and wine goblets, candles and candlesticks. With chairs that have not been upholstered, tie-on seat cushions will add comfort as well as color for relatively little outlay.

CHINA AS A COLOR ACCENT

With so many possibilities made available through different table settings, the danger in dining rooms lies in creating a medley of colors that do not complement each other successfully. A safe starting place and also a necessary consideration in planning your color scheme is your china. If you have multicolored china, remember that you can choose to highlight elsewhere on the table a secondary color in the china's design—in fact, this may be preferable to repeating the main color, which can begin to look too uniform when given too much emphasis. For example, it may be better to pick up as a napkin color the greens of a leaf in a floral pattern than to echo the colors of the flower petals. Another possibility is to choose an accent color that complements the china, such as yellow with blue, or red with green. As always, remember the value of natural colors to break up color, to introduce variety or to form a neutral background on which to base your color scheme.

WALLS AND WINDOWS

Because of the variety of color that can be introduced to the table setting, along with the colors of the food, dining room walls are more often plain than patterned. Intricate wallpaper and curtain designs will work against your focal point, so if you want something more adventurous than a plain background color, consider using a striped paper. Remember, too, that you can introduce contrast to the walls by putting up a dado rail and painting the wall space below the dado a darker shade than the color above it. Look for curtain or blind fabrics that contain both shades.

MAKING THE MOST OF WOOD

Wood is frequently used as a foreground color in dining rooms. Although many synthetic materials are available nowadays, oak, pine and mahogany remain popular choices for tables and chairs. You may choose to extend the theme of wood by having a plain wooden floor, which is an option as practical as it is attractive. You may also choose to strip and varnish the door and window frames, baseboard and mantelpiece, but this is not advisable unless the woodwork is of high quality.

As a general rule, strong colors work well with wood,

ABOVE This small space shows not only how a comfortable eating area can be created in a narrow room, but also how effectively stripes can be used to widen a space. The lines of the floorboards are repeated in the wide, harmonizing stripes of the wallpaper, and the choice of light colors from the air palette adds to the overall effect and provides a contrast to the dark green kitchen beyond.

though the paler neutrals, reminiscent of natural stone or brickwork, also make for handsome companion colors. Dark woods, such as oak, walnut and mahogany, can easily withstand rich, intense shades, while pine, ash and maple rest more comfortably against lighter tints.

Painted wood has long been popular in northern Europe and this popularity has only recently spread to England and North America. A distinct advantage of choosing this option is that you can quickly redeem cheap, second-hand wooden furniture by painting it. If you do decide to paint your own furniture, bear in mind that special paint effects such as dragging and stippling can be very time-consuming. Even the most experienced paint specialists find it takes longer to drag a set of six chairs than to drag all four walls of a spacious reception room. Simple techniques, such as combining two paint colors or using a simple stencil design on a chair back, are easier and quicker to execute.

DIVIDING UP THE WALL SPACE

Panels are an ingenious way to add proportion to a room and allow you to create interesting combinations of color and paint effects— here, dragging and rag rolling. Traditionally, walls were always divided into an uneven number of panels.

YOU WILL NEED:

○ Eggshell paint for the pale base color

○ Scumble glaze mixed in two colors (here, gray and blue)

○ Low-tack masking tape

○ Cloth for ragging

○ Long-bristled dragging brush 4in (10cm) wide

○ Long steel ruler

○ Carpenter's level

CAROLYN'S TIPS

❝ Painting the base color off-white will give a much softer effect to the painted panels. ❞

❝ Do not worry about rubbing out the pencil lines: they add emphasis to the paneled effect. ❞

❝ Painting the panels in two tones of the same color can make a small room look larger. ❞

1. Paint the walls all over with two coats of base-color eggshell paint. Allow to dry thoroughly. Work out where you want to place the panels, allowing approximately 4in (10cm) between them. Draw the panel outlines on the wall, using a soft pencil and the steel ruler. Use the level to check that your lines are straight. Apply masking tape around the edge of each panel to create the border.

2. Brush on the first glaze color with uneven brushstrokes, taking care not to overlap the masking tape edges. Scrunch up the cloth and, using both hands, roll it over the glaze while wet to create a broken effect. The glaze is slow-drying and remains tacky for some time. Finish each panel before starting on the next. Allow to dry thoroughly before moving on to Step 3.

3. Brush a thin layer of the second colored glaze on the wide strips around each panel. Using the dragging brush (which should be the width of the strips), start from the top and drag the brush downwards, applying even pressure and working long, vertical strokes. Do the vertical strips first and then fill in the horizontal areas in the same way, but dragging the brush from left to right, to create the illusion of a wooden panel. Once the glaze is dry, remove the masking tape, to reveal a crisp white or pale-colored border.

ABOVE Used together, the grays and blues of the wind palette create an atmosphere of sophistication and elegance. These paneled walls also include a fine white line that slightly separates and so enhances the interplay of these two colors. The dominance of blue in the tablecloth and chairs brings that color forward, while the use of red as a secondary color contrasts with it and lends a note of brightness.

THE KITCHEN

Even in an era of prepared supermarket meals, the kitchen remains the most functional of rooms. It can also be one of the most magnetic.

Who has not been drawn towards the kitchen by the smell of chicken roasting, stews simmering, bread baking or coffee brewing? Kitchens have to do with smell as much as with sight, and this makes the art of creating a successful kitchen more subtle than it may at first appear. Creating a welcoming kitchen relies on choosing colors that will not compete with the invisible center of the room —the meal that is hidden in the oven, or simmering on top of the stove.

WHITE AS A KITCHEN COLOR

White is an obvious choice for kitchens. It also has the advantage of reflecting light, an important consideration in a place where food is being prepared. However, white used in excess can begin to look clinical and stark, particularly in a large kitchen, or one that does not benefit from much natural light. You can counter this by choosing a lightly tinted beige or a pale gray for your walls and ceiling, particularly if you already have white kitchen units.

PRACTICAL FLOOR SURFACES

Balance pale kitchen walls with a dark, bold floor surface. Stained wood, tiles and stone flags are traditional, hard-wearing surfaces for kitchen floors, but they can be prohibitively expensive. If you want a wooden surface, make sure that it is well varnished and sealed to withstand spillage, and be prepared to have it retreated every other year. A wide variety of good-quality vinyl flooring is now manufactured. As well as being durable and easy to clean, it is also less hard underfoot than traditional kitchen floor surfaces. Remember that a rug laid under a kitchen table can be used as a bridge from the colors of the floor to those used on the walls and table.

LEFT Nothing can transform wooden surfaces as much as a well-chosen paint finish. The pale yellow cupboards of this basement kitchen bring a welcome sense of light and are beautifully complemented by the blue and white window blind and the tiles. The main colors in the room are chosen from the wind palette.

❍ Careful use of space and light, together with natural colors, give this kitchen its distinctive character.

❍ Light–painted woodwork maximizes the natural light and creates a sense of spaciousness.

❍ An eclectic array of brightly colored vases on the windowsill provides a playful accent among the softer shades.

FAR LEFT Using colors of equal intensity from the fire palette creates a dramatic atmosphere in this modern kitchen. Burnt orange walls complement strong lilac-blue units. Black is used for the worktops and baseboards, moderating the impact of the two main colors.

LEFT White-painted woodwork maximizes the natural light and creates a sense of space in this kitchen. Plain work units designed in an L-shape separate the cooking from the eating area. The white theme continues in the choice of china, placemats, table napkins and tulips, showing what a difference attention to detail can make.

THE BLUE KITCHEN

For centuries, cobalt blue was used as a traditional color in kitchens and pantries because this particular shade is repellent to insects. Modern ways of preserving foodstuffs have made considerations such as this less relevant than they once were, but you may like to bear the property of cobalt blue in mind if you are decorating a country kitchen, particularly one in a warm climate.

KITCHEN UNITS

Since the Second World War, kitchen design has passed through more changes of fashion than that of any other room—from the streamlined look of the sixties, with its emphasis on plastics, to the nostalgic, rustic look of the seventies and the rise of the fitted kitchen, now giving way once more to a trend towards free-standing furniture. In all of these variations, a constant factor is the need for smooth surfaces, which provide stable, hygienic worktops. How-ever, these expanses can create a bland, clinical look, especially in a streamlined modern kitchen. One way of countering this is to use a textured paint treatment for your kitchen units. Another is to choose a wood such as ash or maple. High-quality unpainted wood is pleasing to the eye partly because the natural wood grain contributes to a depth of color and a constant, subtle play of light that is absent from synthetic surfaces.

COLOR ACCENTS

With the range of options that are now available, the way you design your kitchen will probably be influenced as much by your temperament as your taste in color. If you are a person who likes your surroundings to be regulated and tidy, a streamlined kitchen, where everything is contained in cupboards, will probably appeal to you more than one where pots and pans, mugs and baskets are hung up for display.

Whichever style you prefer, be aware that the kitchen is an ideal place in which to experiment with color accents. Use the space between upper and lower cabinets for a range of tiles; take advantage of simple, functional objects such as kitchen clocks, storage canisters and dish towels. Pile rosy apples in a black lacquer bowl for a dramatic effect; arrange lemons alongside eggplants and zucchini in round baskets for a splash of exoticism; for a more muted display, combine bananas with a mixture of pears and nuts. Hang up bunches of dried flowers and herbs, ropes of colored candles, strings of garlic. Use the space on top of storage units to display big pieces of pottery and china, such as large vases, meat dishes and soup tureens. All of these accents will lend character to your kitchen without requiring you to make any permanent changes. A well-designed kitchen is colorful without being overpowering, functional without being severe: the kind of space that puts you in mind of good living and makes you look forward to the next meal.

ABOVE Natural colors and a rustic stone effect can make a storage area seem to recede. Here, the cupboards and walls have both been painted as light stonework, introducing a note of humor as well as softening the many sharp angles and corners.

ABOVE A pleated shade is a practical and unobstrusive way of decorating a window. Since it is always pulled up, it maximizes the amount of light allowed in. The discipline of this blue-and-white checked shade is also heightened by the more opaque colors of the vases displayed below it and by the contrast in both design and texture of the blue-and-white tiles.

A cook's view

Make a stunning focal point of a kitchen window with a fake Roman shade and a display shelf running across the width of the window.

1. Cut the wooden batten to the exact width of your window frame and mark its position on the wall just above the top of the window recess, using the level and pencil. Screw securely into place. Apply one side of the hook-and-loop tape, cut to the length of the batten.

YOU WILL NEED:

○ Fabric as wide as window and about half the length

○ Lining fabric of the same dimensions

○ Wooden batten as wide as window frame

○ Self-adhesive hook-and-loop tape (like Velcro)

○ Wooden dowel as wide as the shade

○ Carpenter's level and pencil

2. Cut out the material—first joining widths together, if necessary—to the width of the window frame, adding a 1in (2.5cm) seam allowance on either side. The length should allow for two or three folds, plus 1in (2.5cm) for turnings at top and bottom. Pin right sides together and machine stitch the fabric and lining together on three sides, leaving the top open. Turn right side out and insert the length of doweling at the bottom of the shade to weigh it down; stitch to hold it in place. Slipstitch the opening closed, folding in 1in (2.5cm) hems on both main fabric and lining. Sew the other strip of hook-and-loop tape to the top on the lining side. Fold the fabric to imitate Roman shade folds, as shown, and stitch underneath the folds. Fix the shade in place above the window.

CAROLYN'S TIP

" Fix a wooden shelf across the window recess to create a wonderful display area for glass or other objects, or for a row of indoor plants. "

The Bedroom

Few experiences are more pleasurable than waking up at leisure in a comfortable, beautifully decorated bedroom.

You do not need to go on holiday or stay in a smart hotel to enjoy this experience. It is an affordable luxury that can be encountered on an everyday basis by anyone who takes the trouble to introduce colors, textures and bedroom furnishings that please the eye and relax the senses. Successful bedroom design turns as much on skillful use of color as on any other factor.

The quality that most of us associate with bedrooms is restfulness. Drama certainly plays its part in bedroom design, but in a room that is going to be used every night, the priority is to create a color scheme that is harmonious, well balanced and elegant.

Versatile naturals

Naturals are frequently used to excellent effect in bedrooms of all sizes. A subtle blend of pale, natural colors will quickly create an atmosphere of tranquility. The most frequent error made by inexperienced decorators using naturals is to choose one hue only, and to overlook the effect of its base color. A natural bedroom soon becomes a bland bedroom if you do not pick up and echo the base color. For example, with a light gray, which contains black, choose upholstery and curtain fabric that echo this, however slightly. Pick up an almond natural with dark browns, and a light pink with a deeper scarlet. You can also avoid monotony by introducing a shade that complements the base color—blue with a yellow-base neutral, pinky red to enhance a green base and orange to enhance a purple base. For a soothing effect, stay with very light tints in your choice of colors; for a note of drama, choose one more strongly colored item, such as the bedspread or curtains, as a highlight for the room.

You can also introduce variety to a natural bedroom through your choice of textures. Consider hanging blinds

RIGHT Complementary shades of yellow and purple from the fire palette provide the main colors in this room.

❍ By using complementary colors on the walls, architectural balance is created in an awkward-shaped room.

❍ The foreground colors are more muted, the natural striped fabric of the bedcover echoing and enhancing the slatted woodwork of the bed frame.

❍ Another pair of complementary colors, this time red and blue, have been introduced in the two prints on the right-hand wall, adding to the spirit of the design.

❍ The two side-by-side pictures balance the small window on the adjacent wall.

in a smooth fabric and contrast this with a more loosely woven curtain material, such as calico. Play with different colors and textures by combining different fabrics for your valance, pillowcases, quilt and counterpane. And remember that a layered look will add warmth, so even if you have a wall-to-wall carpet, try laying a rug over it to create this effect.

Dark color accents

Rooms that are decorated with peace and quiet in mind can look unimaginative, even if they have been thoughtfully conceived. To add definition and style to a neutral bedroom, introduce a few dark accents, such as wooden or iron curtain rods and finials, dark mirror frames and an antique bedstead. Avoid heavy woods, however, since their bulk can overpower neutral surroundings.

The green bedroom

The color of transition and the color we most readily associate with nature, green is famous for its restful properties, making it an extremely reliable bedroom color. Another virtue of green is that it appears as a secondary color in

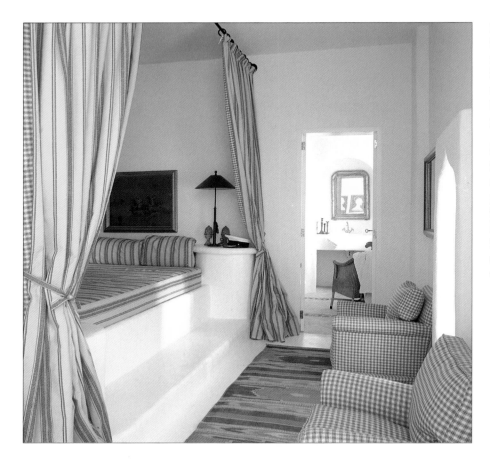

LEFT Assertive on its own, this warm red
from the earth palette becomes more
restrained when it is combined with cream
from the natural palette. The combination
of checks and stripes adds to the visual
interest of the room, as does the richly
patterned bedside rug.

RIGHT This room is a beautiful example of
the use of dark metal for color accents in
a room with a predominantly natural
palette. The palest ivory on the wall is
taken just a few shades darker with the
broadly striped duvet cover, while the
intricate lace pillows create an extremely
effective contrast to the simplicity of the
wrought-iron bedstead, chair and mirror.

numerous floral and abstract wallpapers and soft furnishing fabrics. So green will happily combine with many color schemes in which patterns play a dominant role. Dark green can be too severe in bedrooms, but the mid- to light greens are an excellent foil for floral curtains and bedspreads, or for a highly patterned rug.

SEASONAL CONTRASTS

Before the advent of central heating, it was common practice in many houses to hang warm, interlined curtains, and to use heavy blankets during the winter months and replace these with lighter fabrics when spring returned. There is something inherently pleasing about being in a room that has been decorated in keeping with the weather outdoors and the character of the season, even if the indoor temperature is artificially regulated. By changing thick, warm curtains for light cottons and substituting a heavy bedspread

for a pretty lace throw, you can give your bedroom a new lease on life for the summer months without needing to make any structural alterations.

THE BED AS A CENTERPIECE

The type of bed you have, and the way in which you dress it, plays a leading role in creating the atmosphere of your bedroom. Beds used to be extremely solid pieces of furniture, sometimes even sold as part of the contents of the house when it changed hands. Today, such beds are more luxurious than commonplace, but even an ordinary bed can still become the centerpiece of a bedroom if it is given a fine headboard and an interesting quilt.

Traditional wooden beds, such as the French country beds, call for solid, traditional colors and old-fashioned bedcoverings, such as the patterned quilts that the women of eighteenth- and nineteenth-century North America made into an art form. The lighter wooden bed frames that are on the market today call for lighter colors and fabrics such as Indian cottons, though if you prefer, their wood can be stained to create a darker and more powerful antique effect. For a country look, choose a busy, cottage-garden bedspead or a bright patchwork quilt. For a more restrained, classical atmosphere choose wide, harmonious stripes or a solid color. For a romantic look, combine a brass bedstead with white sheets, a lace coverlet and a pile of lace-trimmed cushions.

CHOOSING BEDROOM FURNITURE

The position of a bed in a room can make a huge difference to the room's overall appearance. In small bedrooms, the bed will be the dominant piece of furniture, and the colors used in covering it will greatly influence the sense of space in the room. Red makes objects stand out from their surroundings, so if you choose this color, the size of the bed will appear to increase. On the other hand, if you choose a strong color for the walls and a lighter shade of the same color for the bed, the bed will harmonize more discreetly with its surroundings.

Larger rooms can seem to be underfurnished if they contain only a bed and a wardrobe or a chest of drawers. These rooms present the opportunity to create a small seating area. With a large bedroom, consider how you may most effectively divide the space—rugs are a simple but successful way of dividing floor space so as to delineate the different parts of a room.

STORAGE

If you have space, a walk-in closet is an excellent way to store clothes and linens. However, a number of contemporary homes feature free-standing wardrobes or prominent

ABOVE Wind colors can create a sunny, welcoming atmosphere, especially when complementary shades are chosen. Here, blue and yellow complement each other beautifully, with wooden furnishings providing a natural accent.

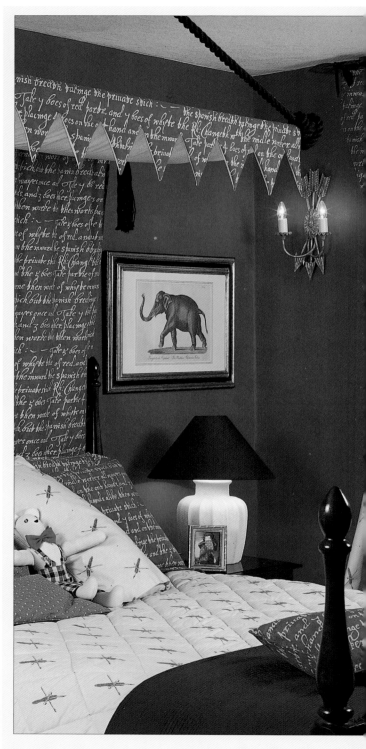

closet designs. The main advantage of floor-to-ceiling storage systems is that they maximize storage space. The drawback is that this can often upset the proportions of a room. One way of countering this is to use special paint effects— highlight the paneling of your closet doors with a color that complements the base color, introduce a stencil design in the panels, or paint the panels a different color than the frame of the closet. Another attractive option is to choose closet frames that are without upper panels and to line them with a simple patterned fabric. This instantly softens the appearance of a room. You also have the chance to coordinate the fabric of the closets with the curtains or with other upholstery materials.

A HARLEQUIN PELMET

An unusual pelmet forms part of the curtain treatment in this bedroom and allows color-coordinated fabrics to be used effectively.

YOU WILL NEED:

○ Pelmet fabric

○ Lining fabric

○ Buckram (stiffened interlining)

○ Brown paper for making a pattern

○ Ribbon or tape for pelmet ties, each one approximately 12in (30cm) long and 1½in (4cm) wide

○ Curtain rod about length of bed width

LEFT The mineral palette can come into its own in basement rooms. But the deep reds that establish the signature color of this bedroom are counterbalanced by natural creams on the curtains, bedspread, lampstands and picture mounts, softening its theatrical quality. Dark blue ropes and lampshades establish definition and a note of masculinity.

1. Measure the curtain pole to determine the length of the pelmet. Decide on the depth of the pelmet and the proportions of the diamonds and draw the whole pattern on brown paper. Add ⅝in (1.5cm) for a seam allowance all around. Calculate the number of ties required and cut them to length.

CAROLYN'S TIPS

❝ Create a matching bed canopy using the same diamond harlequin pattern: make a half-diamond (a triangle) at each edge of a corner. ❞

❝ As a finishing touch or to add an accent color, sew a small tassel to the tip of each diamond. ❞

2. Using the paper pattern as a template, cut out the fabric and lining. Cut the buckram ⅝in (1.5cm) smaller all around. Place the right sides of the fabric and lining together, with the buckram in between. Pin, baste and then machine stitch around the diamonds and the sides of the pelmet, leaving the top edge open. Trim away seam allowances, almost up to the seam line at the lower points of the diamonds, and notch the seam allowance at the inward-facing angles. Turn right side out, using a pencil to push out the points of the diamonds.

3. Mark the position of the ties with pins. Fold the ties in half and pin them in place. Turn in and press ⅝in (1.5cm) on both fabric and lining; pin and then sew the top edges together by hand or machine, enclosing the ties. Remove the pins. Iron the seams, especially the zigzags, then tie the finished pelmet on to the curtain rod.

THE BATHROOM

If we were to decorate other rooms in our homes with the same flair and boldness that we bring to our bathrooms, many of our houses would be a good deal more stylish than they often are.

Whether it is because we spend only short periods of time in them, or because the activity of bathing itself releases our imaginations, we tend as homemakers to bring a more emphatic sense of color to the decoration of our bathrooms than we do to any other room.

The scale of bathrooms also seems to encourage a sense of adventure. In most contemporary homes, bathrooms take up relatively little space, which makes them good places in which to experiment with color. If you make a ghastly mistake, it won't cost very much to set it right and start again, and a small bathroom can be redecorated in a relatively short space of time, compared to most other rooms.

WATER, LIGHT AND COLOR

A room associated specifically with washing, the bathroom has immediate connotations of water. The element of water characteristically changes according to the quality of the light and reflects the colors of everything around it. The decorating color that most effectively enhances this play of light and water is turquoise. True turquoise is midway between blue and green in the color spectrum. Used as a base or a foreground color, it can be combined with white to create a Mediterranean look, and with coral for a Caribbean look. It can also withstand fiery reds and deep greens, creating a South Pacific atmosphere, and can be used with a range of darker blues to emphasize its connection with the sea.

Deep blue and purple are associated with opulence in many cultures, from the lapis lazuli that was prized by the Sumerians and Egyptians to the deep blue glass made by European merchant traders to display their wealth to fellow traders. But the starker, more classical blues can appear

RIGHT Cool Scandinavian summers come to mind in the water colors of this simple blue-and-white bathroom.

❍ Horizontal, blue-painted wooden paneling around the bathtub increases the width of the room and provides convenient shelf space for a collection of starfish.

❍ The graceful white curve of the window is charmingly reflected in the inverted curve of the bath shelf to its left.

❍ Dark blue tongue-and-groove paintwork on the side of the bath and the basin cabinet offset the paler paneling above the bath.

❍ Blue and white ornaments, a white lampshade and a white chair continue the discipline, making a virtue of simplicity. It is hard to imagine introducing a third color to this scheme without detracting from the overall effect.

cold if they are used over large surfaces. A more pleasing effect is often achieved by working with blues that contain a hint of green, taking them closer to turquoise, or of red, which shifts their hue towards purple.

THE WHITE BATHROOM

White is a popular choice for bathrooms, associated as it is not only with light on water but also with cleanliness, and it is the traditional color for bathtubs, sinks and toilets. One of the chief merits of white is its versatility. Its brilliance can be emphasized by bright chrome or brass fittings and by contrasting dark woods and strong base colors. As a base color itself, it can be made more playful by introducing bright color accents with soaps and towels, curtains, blinds and pictures. For a more sophisticated bathroom, use a very light gray as a wall color rather than plain white; for a more light-hearted atmosphere choose a light cream, and for a romantic bathroom, try white that contains a blush of pink.

LEFT Make the most of a collection of china with a coordinating wallpaper. No space is wasted in this small bathroom—even the top of the window frame is adorned with vases. Because colors from the wind palette are used in both the wallpaper and the china, and because most of the items are small in scale, the space is made to seem larger than it actually is. The large mirror above the sink also increases the room's apparent size.

BELOW *Trompe l'oeil* tiles are created by painting gray lines and a small corner motif on this bathroom cabinet.

MIRRORS AND TILES

In a bathroom setting, mirrors and tiles share three main qualities—they are economical, they are practical and they are decorative. The tiles you choose can set the theme for the rest of your bathroom, and if you select a multicolored design, you will have more than one option to work with. It pays to research the many tiles that are now on the market. If you are working with a tight budget and come across an expensive pattern, try combining it with cheaper, plain tiles so that you can use it over a wide area. You may also like to try using a stencil design to create a *trompe l'oeil* tiling effect.

As well as performing a practical function, mirrors can be made a design feature of any bathroom. In a small space, large mirrors are an invaluable way of increasing the apparent size of a room. Strategically placed, they can also intensify the use of color highlights. Avoid placing your bathroom mirror directly opposite a door, otherwise you

will not be maximizing its effectiveness. Try experimenting with a small piece of mirror, such as a mirrored tile, by holding it up at different levels. It is often hard to assess the scope of a mirror before you hang it, so it pays to experiment. You will enhance the play of color and light in your bathroom if you use mirrors on more than one wall, particularly if you line three walls at right angles to one another, so that the glass reflects the colors on the opposite wall in different ways.

WALLPAPER

Using wallpaper is an easy way of giving extra character to a bathroom. Striped wallpapers will give you a classical, townhouse look, while a floral pattern will create a more traditional, romantic atmosphere. Alternatively, you can create a more fantastic atmosphere with a design that features gold or silver, and combine this with a dark floor treatment. For a tentlike effect, take your paper design

LEFT Natural colors prevail in this simple and economically decorated bathroom. The nostalgic look of the old-fashioned tub continues with the fine white lace of the curtain, which in its turn softens the shuttered window frame. Discreet accents from the water palette in the overhead light fitting and the shutters bring just the right note of freshness to complete the effect.

ABOVE The rich colors of the mineral palette can turn an ordinary bathroom into something special. Here, the matt finish of the stonework-effect walls contrasts effectively with the sheen of the tiles behind the bath.

across the ceiling as well as the walls. Before you invest in wallpaper for a bathroom, check with the retailer to ensure that it is steam-proof and washable, otherwise you may need to apply a coat of matt varnish to the walls.

ENSUITE BATHROOMS

An ensuite bathroom can either contrast or harmonize with the bedroom to which it connects. Whichever is your preference, take care when you are selecting your bathroom colors to compare them to the bedroom colors on a sample board. A small bathroom alongside a more spacious bedroom involves a significant shift of scale and if you combine this with too dramatic a shift of color, you may create a contrast that is more overpowering than you intend.

STONEWORK WALLS

The mystery of ancient civilizations is evoked in the rustic *trompe l'oeil* stonework finish on the walls of this bathroom, shown in close-up detail, left. Careful blending of the three colors chosen from the mineral palette creates an authentic stone effect. Use a natural sponge to blend the colors together.

YOU WILL NEED:

○ Graph paper

○ Steel ruler

○ Carpenter's level

○ Eggshell paint for basecoat

○ Scumble glaze in 3 colors (here, mineral shades of red, terracotta and brown)

○ 2 natural sea sponges, one cut into 3 pieces

○ Low-tack masking tape ¼ in (50mm) wide

○ Paint roller and small paintbrush

1. Apply two coats of eggshell basecoat paint to the walls, using a roller, and allow to dry. Measure your walls and work out the stonework pattern to scale on graph paper, staggering the joints. As a rough guide, standard stone blocks are 1ft (30cm) high and 2ft (60cm) wide; try to use only whole or half blocks across a row. Transfer the scaled-up measurements to the walls using the steel ruler, level and a pencil. Mask off the edges of each complete block with masking tape.

2. Rinse the sponges in cold water and squeeze out excess water. Using a separate piece of sponge for each color, dab on a random mix of all three stonework colors, overlapping the patches of color. Start from the top and work down. While still wet, use the sponge and paintbrush to blend the colors together to create the stonework effect. Do each block in turn. The more random the effect of each block, the greater the illusion of natural stone.

3. Once you have finished all the blocks and the paint is dry, carefully remove the masking tape to reveal instant grout lines. If desired, apply two coats of a matt-finish clear varnish for protection.

CAROLYN'S TIPS

❝ Paint the basecoat a beige/yellow color to give the grouting a realistic touch. ❞

❝ For a more 'antique' look, hand-drawn lines can be added using a thin artist's brush to give the effect of cracks in the stone. ❞

❝ Colors from the natural palette combine to give an effective 'stone-colored' wall— look at natural stone- and brickwork for inspiration. ❞

CHILDREN'S ROOMS

The customized decoration of children's rooms is a relatively recent phenomenon. For centuries, children were perceived as "little adults," and while items of furniture such as cribs, chairs and desks were made to scale for children, the notion of a particular decorative style for children's rooms, as with children's clothes, did not gain currency until the Victorian period.

Since that time, a steadily increasing range of enchanting wallpapers and furnishing fabrics have been produced with the world of the child in mind. To some extent, this movement has now been bastardized by the widespread merchandising of children's characters on soft furnishing products. Even so, today's parents face a multitude of options in decorating a child's room.

INFANCY

Infancy is traditionally associated with white, as the color representing new life and innocence. With a newborn baby, it is difficult not to be captivated by the prospect of a tiny cradle with fine white drapes. It is as though the magical quality of the first months of life is somehow extended by placing the baby in surroundings that are specifically intended to celebrate its arrival. Magic aside, an advantage to using white as the base color in a newborn baby's nursery is that you can easily paint over it as the child grows and you want to introduce stronger themes. If white seems too plain, try choosing a pale pastel color and providing interest with a wallpaper or stencil frieze, patterned curtains and a crewel rug.

Although newborn babies cannot focus properly, they do sense the quality of their surroundings from a very early age. So take the trouble to prepare your baby's room in advance of the birth, and aim to create a color scheme that you feel will provide your baby with a sense of security and well-being. Modern babies seem to acquire a great deal of

RIGHT Busy patterns, brightly painted woodwork and a warm background color, all from the earth palette, set the tone for this girl's bedroom.

❍ A lick of paint—cream, red and pale blue—has transformed the bedside table and chest of drawers, while fabric panels in the same colors give a facelift to the wardrobe.

❍ Three fabrics with contrasting patterns and harmonizing colors combine to create subtle and playful contrasts between the curtains, blinds and bed covers.

❍ The warmth that is inherent in the red of this fabric is amplified by the red paintwork on the walls. A quite different atmosphere would have been created with blue or yellow paint.

❍ With these busy fabric designs, the simplest coir matting easily suffices as floorcovering.

apparatus within the first weeks of life and many stores now offer customized nursery sets comprising a changing table, crib and chest of drawers—so you may want to make these items the starting point for your decoration.

PRESCHOOL CHILDREN

Preschool children spend much of their day at home and their bedrooms are as likely to be used for playing in as for sleeping in. During this critical period of your child's growth, your concern is likely to center on how best to engage your child's interest in the world around him or her. Small children are insatiably curious, and by the age of two they are beginning to develop a conscious sense of pattern, shape and color. There are all sorts of ways in which you can foster this blossoming awareness, not only with toys but also with patterned wallpapers, playmats, duvet covers and curtains.

There is a widespread assumption that small children most appreciate primary colors and simple patterns, but in

LEFT The light green paint that provides the background color for this bedroom runs right across the ceiling as well as the walls, increasing the sense of space. Green from the water palette is stylishly offset by its complementary color, red, from the fire palette, on the baseboard, radiator and bed base. But the most notable feature of this bedroom is the window. By using vivid red and yellow stripes on the frame, a red shade and a cheap and cheerful Indian hanging, the creator of this room has turned an ordinary window into a visual feast.

fact children can have quite a sophisticated sense of color and pattern from a very early age. If you decorate a toddler's room in raw yellows, reds, and blues, he is likely to be bored by it as soon as you are. If you think back to your own childhood, you may well find that you have a particular memory of the pattern on the wallpaper or a carpet. Young children enjoy intricacy and they live in close contact with the floor. Carpets with interesting lines and curves double as roads, rivers and exotic landscapes. Cur-

tains that fall to the floor provide hiding places and create interesting pools of light for a child to explore, while detailed patchwork quilts provide a starting point from which a child can begin to spin his or her own stories.

PRIMARY SCHOOL CHILDREN

Once children start school, they are beginning to stake their claim on the look of their room. They may well want to use their bedroom walls for their own paintings, drawings and

LEFT Bright fire colors and simple but clever designs make this bedroom an ideal setting for a young child's adventures. A broad frieze lowers the ceiling, bringing the scale of the room down to become more child-centred. *Trompe l'oeil* cubes make the bed into a play area in its own right and cleverly camouflage two drawers.

LEFT Storage space for children's toys presents a challenge that is all too often dealt with by storing the toys out of sight. This bright checkerboard pattern from the water palette shows how the challenge can be addressed openly and made into an eye-catching feature of a child's room.

collections. Your main concern now is probably that the carpet will be hard-wearing and all surfaces easy to clean. For this age group, the decorating that is most appreciated is the kind that fosters imaginative play—making your child a bed that is like a boat, or a wardrobe that doubles as a sentry box, will delight him or her far more than expensive designer curtain fabric. If you do not have the skill or the budget to create a specially designed bed, consider painting your child's furniture. It is very easy to pick up cheap, second-hand chests of drawers that can be transformed by a set of stencils into a jungle or farmyard scene. A customized piece of furniture can also become a treasured memento of younger days when your child is older.

COLORS FOR BOYS, COLORS FOR GIRLS

As a culture, we still associate blue with boys and pink with girls, despite the fact that these colors may do little or nothing for many children of either sex. Indeed, it is said that babies notice primary colors first. You can learn about your child's preferences by playing games that involve choosing colors and noticing which are the favorites. For a room that will work well for children of both sexes, avoid stereotypical colors such as pink, and fabrics that are overtly masculine or feminine in their design. Yellow is always a safe choice as a background color for a small child's room—think of using check or striped curtains that will go with the different furnishings as a child progresses from a crib to a bed. Changing a duvet cover is always a simple and quick way of giving the room a new look. Abstract patterns, or animal patterns, combined with rich, earthy colors are entirely appropriate for children of both sexes.

TEENAGERS

The bedroom is more often than not the only part of the house that your teenager can claim as his or her own. It will be a sanctuary; the place to which he or she retreats to plan and to read; to rock the house with music and to conspire with friends. Whatever your notion of the perfect teenage bedroom, you can be sure that teens will have strong views on the matter as well. Let them have their say. To be adolescent is to experiment, so if your thirteen-year-old daughter wants lime green and orange cubes on her bedroom walls, she will have her own special reasons for that choice. If your sixteen-year-old son insists that his bedroom is painted deep purple, it may be simplest to let him have his own way.

With children of any age, decorating can raise so many issues that the room goes to the bottom of your priorities and remains unchanged, year after year. Try not to let the difficulties drive you into opting out altogether. A very simple idea, such as a frieze round the dado of a preschool child's bedroom, or floral curtains and a proper dressing table for a ten-year-old girl, will help them to appreciate and enjoy their own space and to feel valued and special at the same time.

CAROLYN'S TIP

❝ Do not worry if some images seem darker than others. Leave it until the border is completed and take an overall view of the wall. Any obvious differences can always be corrected, but bear in mind that these variations can give a charming, hand-finished look to your work. ❞

HOME SWEET HOME

This stenciled frieze takes inspiration from the design on the rug, using reversed colors. The frieze lowers the ceiling and lends interest to what would otherwise be quite a stark white wall space. The choice of blue from the wind palette with natural white creates a crisp but at the same time inviting atmosphere. Warmth is added by the golden tones of the wooden furnishings and floorboards.

YOU WILL NEED:

○ Ready-made stencil (or you can make your own to echo a motif in the room)

○ Low-tack masking tape

○ Nondrip stencil paints

○ A stencil brush for each color

○ Steel ruler

○ Carpenter's level

○ Pencil

1. Work out where you are going to place the stencil. Try to line it up with something in the room, such as the curtain pole here. Using the ruler and level, mark pencil lines on the wall to ensure that your frieze runs in a straight line.

2. Stick the stencil to the wall with masking tape around the edges. Start in the center of the wall and work to the right and then to the left corners. Work out how many images will fit between the center and the corner; alway leave more space between the last few images to fill a small gap to a corner, rather than using half an image.

3. Using the stencil brush, fill in the main color (blue) first, moving the stencil along the wall as you complete each one. It may be possible to paint another color at the same time, using a different brush, provided it is not adjacent to the main color. Try to ensure that no paint goes under the stencil.

4. Once the first color is dry, line up the stencil for the next color (here, ocher), and fill it in using a separate stencil brush.

THE HOME OFFICE

Economic benefits such as reduced rent, lower overheads and no commuting have made working from home, on either a part- or a full-time basis, an increasingly attractive option for many people.

The postwar era has seen a major shift from an industrialized world to one that is more and more dominated by information technology. This revolution is enabling a growing number of individuals to communicate long-distance from desktop to desktop in a way that is unprecedented.

PLANNING PERMISSION AND SAFETY REGULATIONS

Before you embark on the conversion of a particular room or outbuilding into a home office, it is essential to check your local zoning laws. Some suburban districts simply do not allow the practice of certain businesses from home if they are likely to disrupt the peace of the neighborhood. If you will have to enlarge or renovate your home to make an office space, make sure that you have the appropriate permits before you start.

Once you are registered as working from home, industry health and safety standards will apply. Take the trouble to find out what the requirements are, both on your own account and also on behalf of anyone you may be employing to work from your home.

SPACE AND COLOR

If you are working or plan to work from home, a primary consideration will be space. You may be fortunate enough to live in a house that has plenty of room to spare for the creation of a home office, but if this is not the case, choosing a room to work in will probably mean sacrificing a bedroom or den. For most professionals, work involves three different space requirements: space for undisturbed work, space for meetings and space for the storage of documents. You can go out of the home for storage,

RIGHT If you work from home, it is well worth taking the trouble to design an office that is comfortable as well as practical. Warm wind colors have been used to create this stylish home office.

❍ Streamlined wooden furniture and shelving creates a natural, uncluttered look.

❍ Pale paintwork on the walls and ceiling continue the natural theme in a simple and unobtrusive way.

❍ Coir matting provides a practical, hard-wearing floor surface that harmonizes with the wooden furniture.

❍ The upper bookshelf runs right round the room, making good use of what would otherwise be wasted space.

❍ The wide floral shade introduces a feminine note.

❍ The same floral fabric is repeated on the cushion of the armchair, which hints at comfort.

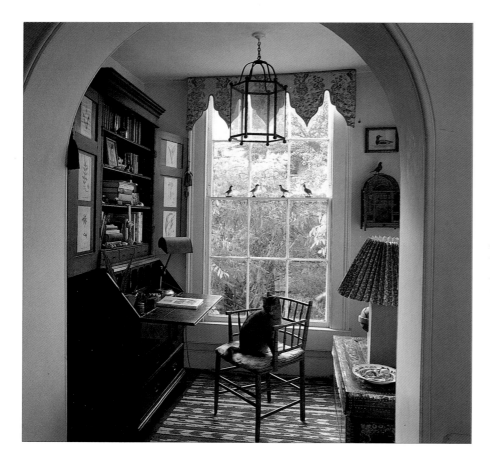

LEFT Dark and light earth colors work together in this tiny study. A modest alcove has become a workplace in its own right with the introduction of a magnificent antique desk and matching bookcase. The pale lemon walls offset the dark wood of the bureau and the trunk opposite it, while the patterns on the ikat-weave rug, paisley lampshade and pelmet break up the areas of solid color.

RIGHT A natural background palette with red accents from the fire palette give this home office a crisp and streamlined appearance. A gray carpet and white on the walls and ceiling increase the sense of space and the splashes of red introduce brightness and warmth.

and if you have company documents you should do so to protect them from fire; you may also be able to run your professional life so that you do not have meetings from home. If you do want to use the house for occasional meetings, consider letting your dining room double as a conference room.

In a house with limited space, it can be tempting to choose the smallest room as the office. This has many advantages: your heat, light and power bills will be correspondingly lower and if you are the kind of person who likes the feeling of working in a cocoon, having a small, cozy workplace can be very pleasant. On the other hand, if you enjoy and need plenty of room in which to spread out, you will probably regret trying to squeeze all of your work material into a tiny attic or basement, particularly if you are working from home on a full-time basis.

When you are setting yourself up at home, it pays to

think ahead. How much space will you need three years from now? It is better to start with lots of space and steadily fill it, than to find you have to move to another part of the house to give yourself the space you need.

Corporate offices tend to be severe and clinical environments, but it is increasingly being recognized that people perform better in an atmosphere that affords some expression of character. Most office equipment will do little to improve the aesthetics of your workplace, so you need to make the most of any opportunities you have to introduce a sense of style to your surroundings. In a small room, you will probably need every inch of space for work-related material. Even so, you can create a play of color by using contrasting colors for bookshelves and the wallspace behind them, hanging lots of pictures close together on any free wall space and laying a kilim or dhurrie on the floor.

LEFT Sewing is an activity that requires a strong light source. Here, cool air colors and lightweight blinds maximize the natural light, while the choice of yellow as the signature color imbues the whole room with a sunny atmosphere.

In a larger office, it is possible to introduce bold color statements and add comfort with pictures, prints or mirrors on the walls, an interesting array of objects on the mantelpiece and throw pillows on an easy chair or sofa. For a warm, womblike atmosphere, choose a base color that is dark, such as a deep red, green or burnt orange, and complement it with a dark wooden desk and shelving units. For a more airy atmosphere, stay with naturals and restrict darker colors to the floor. As in other rooms, bear in mind that an office with plenty of natural light will look good painted in a bright or neutral color, while a darker space will respond well to deeper shades.

WINDOW TREATMENTS

However small your office, you can introduce a degree of individuality through the kind of window treatment you choose. Curtains will take up more space than shades, though they will also make the room less formal. If you have a period home, you may be able to decorate with fitted shutters; in a more modern house, you can choose from a wide variety of shades and blinds. One of the pleasures of having a shade is that you can use it to create a play of light in the daytime, depending on the level to which you draw it down. If you have fabrics or books in your office that will fade with exposure to sunlight, a shade or blind will be practical as well as decorative.

If you do work from home, you will spend more time in your office than in any other part of the house. A comfortable workplace will make a significant difference to the quality of your life. So it is well worth going to a little extra trouble and expense to make your home office a room that you actively enjoy.

1. Apply two coats of basecoat paint with a roller or paintbrush and allow it to dry. Then measure the width of the wall and divide it evenly into stripes. Beware of making the stripes too narrow or the overall effect will be very busy (the stripes here are about 6in/15cm wide). Mark out the stripes by snapping a chalk plumbline against the wall or use a conventional plumbline and draw a light pencil line. Apply masking tape along the lines, placing the tape on the outside edges of the stripes to be painted.

PAINTED STRIPED WALLS

The effect of bright yellow stripes painted on a white background makes a striking wall pattern at a fraction of the cost of wallpaper.

CAROLYN'S TIPS

❝ Try painting two different but harmonious shades of the same color for a soft, two-dimensional tonal effect. ❞

❝ Omit the masking tape and rely on your eye and a steady brush-stroke if you want your stripes to have a more hand-finished edge. ❞

YOU WILL NEED:

○ Basecoat paint for the walls

○ Roller or paintbrush

○ Paint color for the stripes

○ Wide paintbrush

○ Chalk plumbline or plumbline and pencil

○ Low-tack masking tape

2. Paint the stripes with the wide paintbrush. Start at the top and work downwards, making swift brushstrokes. Take care not to overlap the edges of the masking tape. When the paint is dry, carefully remove the masking tape.

WHICH ELEMENT ARE YOU?

The questions here are based on the kind of choices anyone decorating a home has to make. First think about what color means to you by completing "The Real You" (below). Then look carefully at the color choices on the facing page and decide which you prefer. Your answers (see page 128) will determine whether you should select warm- or cool-based palettes for your color schemes. Turn back to the color sections on pages 20–61, looking at either the warm or the cool color wheels. The palette with most of the colors you like to live with determines your element—Air, Wind, Water, Fire, Earth or Mineral. Naturals can be used with all the palettes or on their own.

THE REAL YOU

1. What are your favorite colors?

....

2. What are your least favorite colors?

....

3. How important is home decoration to you?

....

4. Consider the colors you live with now. Are you happy with them?

....

5. Are there other colors you would prefer to live with?

....

6. Do you find yourself always choosing the same colors?

....

7. Have you ever wanted a room in a particular color, and then found you did not like it?

....

8. If you decorated a room and were not satisfied with it, could you manage to live with it or would you feel it had to be changed?

....

9. Which decorating style do you feel happiest in?

....

10. Do the colors in your home reflect some of the colors you like to wear?

....

1. Natural tones are simple and understated. Which of these shades would you choose?

2. You are looking for a versatile, neutral color for the carpet of a hall and staircase. Which of the these do you prefer?

3. Reds create a dramatic and stimulating effect in halls and dining rooms. Which of these shades most appeals to you?

4. Blue rooms can be very restful. Which of these blues would you prefer to use in a blue color scheme?

5. You want to introduce green fabrics into your living room color scheme. Which green would you select?

6. You want to brighten up a dark kitchen. Which of these yellows would you prefer to cook with?

7. Which of these colors would you find most restful to sleep with?

8. Introducing bright colors to a white room creates a bright, Mediterranean atmosphere. Which would you choose as the main color?

9. You are decorating a guest room with a pink theme. On which of these shades would you base the color scheme?

10. You love the aqua colors of the sea. Which shade appeals to you most?

11. You have a dining room to decorate and want to reflect the color of red wine. Which do you prefer?

12. Which of these two colors do you prefer?

Turn to page 128 for the answers.

INDEX

WHICH ELEMENT ARE YOU?

Answers to the questions on pages 124–25:

If most of your answers are **A**s, you are a warm-based person, and should use colors that have yellow undertones. The warm color wheels reflect your colors. If most of your answers are **B**s, this means you are a cool-based person and should use colors with blue undertones, as illustrated in the cool color wheels.

Now turn to pages 20–56 and look at the warm and cool color wheels in all the different palettes. The one that contains the greatest number of colors you would like to use in your home determines which "element" you are.

However, it is important to feel free to mix and match, to use colors from other palettes too. If you are cool and like a particular warm color, or vice versa, then use it for details and accents.

AUTHOR'S ACKNOWLEDGMENTS

Writing this book and developing the *Living with Color* concept has been the most fascinating voyage of discovery into the world of color. Many people have helped and contributed to my work and research. My special thanks go to: Tessa Strickland, my co-author, for her unique skill in interpreting my thoughts and words; Jill Strieder for her constant encouragement and advice; Suzi Pickles for teaching me all about color analysis; Anthony Evans for his invaluable assistance in researching fabric sources; Ruth Churchman for her insight into color.

I would also like to thank the following fabric manufacturers: Malabar, Colefax & Fowler, and Bernard Thorp for the fabrics used in my living room (page 84), C.F. Deanswood Ltd. for making the curtains and upholstery; Jane Churchill Ltd. for the dining room tablecloth fabric (page 93); Colefax & Fowler for the kitchen shade fabric (page 99), as well as M.S. Bloomfield Ltd. for the kitchen units.

This book would not have been possible without the wonderful support of our literary agent, Maggie Noach, and Polly Powell and the team at HarperCollins. I am also very grateful to Nancy Traversy for letting us take photographs in her beautiful home.

A special debt of gratitude goes to Sue Hoggard for all her support and for looking after Jamie and Geordie so brilliantly. A big thank you too to Paula and Claire for all their help. Nothing, however, would have been possible without the love, guidance and inspiration of Francis—the best husband I could ever have.

PICTURE CREDITS

The publishers wish to thank the following photographers and organizations for their kind permission to reproduce the following images:

Robin Allison Smith, 14(b) / Laura Ashley, 30, 115(t) / Bauhaus-Archiv, 10 / Bery Designs, 28–29 / Camera Press, 54, 75, 90, 118–119, 122 / Crowson Fabrics Ltd., 113 / Wendy A. Cushing Ltd., 120–121 / The English Stamp Company, 48–49 / Robert Harding Syndication/IPC Magazines, 18, 24–25, 56–57, 67, 68–69, 80–81, 84–85, 132–133 / The Interior World/Simon Brown, 49, 82, 83, 85, 92 / James Mortimer, 14(cl), 82, 91 / Fritz Von Der Schulenburg, 8–9, 12–13, 20–21, 36–37, 44, 52–53, 104–105, 106, 124–125, 128–129, 136–137 / (Kath Kidson), 17 / (Dot Spikings), 25(r), 97 / (Richard Mudditt), 25, 31, 97 / (Nessa O'Neill), 37 / (Mimmi O'Connell), 66 / (K. H. Scherer), 71 / (Julia Boston), 88–89/ (Juliette Mole), 114 / (Richard Hudson), 123 / Christopher Simon Sykes, 15(tl) / Woloszynski, 43, 55, 64, 70, 102, 120 / Maison de Marie Claire/Gilles de Chabaniex/C de Chabaniex/Bastit, 40–41, 91 / Gaillard/Comte Moireau, 116–117 / Mulberry/Guy Hervais, 60 / Mike Newton, 12(t), 14(cr&tl), 15(b), 68, 121 / David Parmiter, 98 / David Phelps, 24, 69, 76, 101 / Ianthe Ruthven, 84–85 / Paul Ryan/International Interiors, 96–97 / Christian Sarramon (Masurel), 19 / Elizabeth Whiting & Associates, 1, 16 / Coté Sud (C. Dugied), 109 / Coté Sud (Y. Duronsoy), 11 / Coté Sud (B. Touillon), 10, 77 / Coté Ouest (J. Darblay)/Rodney Hyatt, 96, 116–117 / Di Lewis, 14(tr), 42 / Michael Nicholson, 12(b), 15(tr).

Photographs on the following pages were specially taken for HarperCollins by Shona Wood: 20, 26, 32, 38, 44, 48, 50, 78, 80–81, 83, 84, 86, 92–93, 94–95, 98–99, 103, 104, 108, 110, 115(b).